Financial Management for Your Mental Health Practice: Key Concepts Made Simple

Financial Management for Your Mental Health Practice: Key Concepts Made Simple

Jeffrey Zimmerman, Ph.D. and Diane Libby, CPA

ISBN: 0990344533
ISBN 13: 9780990344537
Library of Congress Control Number: 2015918277
TPI Press. The Practice Institute, LLC, Camp Hill PA

Dedication

To Lauren who always supports me and believes in the power of the universe and reaching beyond our comfort zones.
—Jeffrey Zimmerman
To Mark who always encourages me to follow my dreams and is always there to share them with me.
—Diane Libby

Contents

Acknowledgments

Countless colleagues, professional clients, and students have challenged us by asking the questions that inspired us to consider writing this book. We also want to thank our friends at TPI Press who saw the importance of bringing an interdisciplinary (accountant and mental health professional) team together as authors.

However, this book could not have been written without our acknowledging the mistakes and potholes that our colleagues and we have fallen into over the past 30 years. These mistakes have taught us more than we ever learned in our professional training programs. We hope you can take advantage of these lessons with less pain than your predecessors as we try in this book to present the lessons in a practical and readable format.

Our copyeditor Elizabeth Budd has also been a great help to us. She has helped make this book readable and helped us turn some confusing principles into concepts that we hope make sense to you and can be usable going forward.

Lastly, we want to thank our families for their support and encouragement.

Introduction

Get ready to start on a journey. This is a journey you may believe that you just cannot take. Or it may be one that you have attempted but then given up on. The journey is learning some basic accounting and financial business principles and practices as they relate to the operation of a mental health practice.

No, you don't have to be good in math or have an MBA as a prerequisite to begin this journey. We (a psychologist who has spent more than 30 years in private practice and an accountant who consults with mental health practices) are going to teach you the basics in a manner that is straight to the point and pertinent to running an independent mental health practice. Whether you are in solo practice or have a large interdisciplinary practice (or are somewhere in between), we have written this book to help you think about your practice as a business and better understand some of the basic accounting and financial principles necessary to be fiscally aware. It is going to be easier than you expect.

Learning these principles can help you (a) make better business decisions, (b) deal with bank and loan officers, and (c) understand the reports generated by your office software and your accountant. We have purposely kept this book short. It is only seven chapters. Each chapter discusses a key element related to the journey (a stop along the way) and concludes with how all the points in the chapter can fit together.

We begin in Chapter 1 by focusing on why this all seems so difficult. In Chapter 2, we discuss some basic principles of accounting and finance. We show you in Chapter 3 many key measures related to your practice and how you can use them to understand and, when necessary, adjust what is happening in the business of your practice. In Chapter 4, we describe how to use some of these measures and combine them with general, and some specific, strategies for managing your practice. Chapter 5 outlines various strategies for compensating employees and how to determine what ranges of compensation are reasonable for your particular practice. Chapter 6 focuses on planning for retirement. Chapter 7 addresses a number of common business decisions that practice owners face and how to line up your mentors and advisors.

We will give you many ideas and suggestions to consider, but please keep in mind that they are based on 2015 tax laws and other pertinent information. Pension and tax laws change often, and you should always check with your accountant or pension administrator to determine which current laws are in effect. We cannot provide professional tax advice, nor should you consider this book a substitute for professional advice from your own tax, accounting, or legal professionals.

So come join us as we cover what was not taught in graduate school, and do so without having you sit through lecture after lecture. We will take you step by step into and through the ABCs of accounting and financial management of your mental health practice. Who knows? Maybe after reading this book, you will figure out how to give yourself a raise. Wouldn't that be wonderful!

one

I Never Took an Accounting Class

"Accounting 101? Ugh. Why would I want to take that course?"

"I've never been good in math."

"Profit and loss statements, balance sheets, debits, credits—they make my head spin. And what is a *pro forma* anyway?"

"I'm in practice to help people. Why would I need to know that accounting stuff? That's why I have an accountant."

Do these words sound familiar? They certainly are to us as we help mental health clinicians address the financial aspects of running their practices. Many hope the financial side of their practice will take care of itself as they focus on providing the services they specialize in providing. Unfortunately, this is not the case. In fact, the financial side of your practice needs attention and fine-tuning. Businesses do not run on automatic pilot.

Your practice is a business (whether you conceptualize it that way or not). Instead of having a tangible product to deliver, you provide a service. Income is produced when you provide the service. You also have expenses associated with delivering this service. The difference between the income and expenses (called the *net income*) is what is yours to take home.

Many clinicians do not think about their practice as a business for a number of reasons. For example, unlike many businesses, you may not have sought out venture capital for your start-up or even put in much cash up front. Many clinicians begin their practice in a prudent manner by simply renting part-time office space and possibly buying (or renting) a bit of furniture. So, unlike being a typical start-up company, it can seem that you just started to see some clients and put one foot in front of the other until—Poof!—a real practice or business has developed. It is easy to believe that you really haven't made much of a financial investment in your business.

This concept is an illusion. The fact is that there was a tremendous investment to start your practice business. Even if we do not count college, the costs (financially and in the time and energy spent) of your graduate training are key investments. Your training is essential to being able to be licensed so you can be in practice. Added to that figure are the costs of continuing education, taxes, office space, and an infrastructure for running your practice.

Your practice may have an added financial importance. In addition to the amount you have invested (and the psychological and emotional investment), your practice may be the primary financial vehicle that supports your lifestyle. This is different from investing in a mutual fund or stock or buying a piece of real estate, as the revenue generated from your practice may be the only source of funds that ultimately become the major funding of your retirement.

How much income it produces can be directly related to how well it is managed from a business perspective, coupled with the quality of the clinical services provided. Unfortunately, traditional training of mental health professionals focuses only on the latter concept (service delivery) and not the former (financial management and practice development). This leads to critical problems in the viability of many practices, as only half of the essential elements of running a sound professional practice are being addressed by the owner(s) in either the training or skill development related to having a successful business.

Imagine if we asked you to take a substantial sum of money and invest it in a business (other than your practice). We will make the assumption that the business has a good-quality product or service. You think it has potential. Now we say that the owner of the business has little to no training or experience in financial and business management. Are you likely to sign the check over to this person? Your business deserves to have at least the same standard applied to it as you would apply to another investment. You have spent years training and working for this opportunity. You may have invested in your own long-term therapy to help you address your personal issues and minimize the potential for them to have a negative impact on the services you provide. You have likely made many personal sacrifices to begin this business, and we think it is crucial that you give its leadership (i.e., you) the same tools you would look for if the practice were an external investment.

Why Is It So Difficult?

The short answer is, "It isn't really so difficult. It just seems so." It seems this way as a result of a number of factors, including the following.

We clinicians don't typically think this way. One might argue that people who are at their core interested in providing human services are not wired to think from a business perspective. We want to be altruistic (Barnett, Zimmerman, & Walfish, 2014), and we are doing this type of work to help others. This is different from someone who, for example, runs a hedge fund for the sole purpose of making money. It can easily seem that focusing on the business aspects of practice are not essential when compared with the (at times lifesaving) importance of the services being provided. Yet a practice that is a healthy business provides the environment for the clinical services to be delivered in a sustainable fashion. Most clinicians would not be able to provide the services if the practice did not generate income (or a profit) for themselves.

There are strong social pressures to avoid focusing on the business. In some training programs, independent practice is actually strongly discouraged. It is often portrayed as "selling out" or giving up one's soul simply to make money. This may be especially the case in clinical-science psychology programs where the focus is on training researchers or social work programs where the focus is placed on social justice issues. We believe that earning a living providing the services you are trained to provide is not at all selling out. It is honorable and often difficult work. Indeed, although you are being paid to provide services, the work is very special in nature.

We believe we are disempowered. Many trainees and mental health professionals are given (or have developed) a clear message that independent practice is "dead" and that managed care and insurance companies have made it all but impossible for clinicians to have a successful practice. Students and early-career professionals have a sense of learned helplessness about this and see themselves as powerless to influence their earning potential. Yet this common perception is a myth. There are many successful practices (Verhaagen & Gaskill, 2014) and ways to successfully practice outside of managed care (Le & Walfish, 2007; Walfish, 2001, 2010, 2011). An informal survey (by one of the authors) of what help more than 100 mental health professionals needed with their practices resulted in many respondents stating that they were doing fine and were happy. It clearly is possible to have a successful practice.

We think the math is too difficult. We may assume that we need complex math skills or an MBA to run a practice. However, this is not the case. As you'll see in this book, you need only basic math and analytical skills. Some accounting terminology may sound unfamiliar at first, but you'll find that it can be surprisingly simple when applied to your practice.

We think hiring an accountant will solve the problem. Hiring an accountant is often essential to running your practice, and also to making sure you are in compliance with a variety of regulations and tax responsibilities that you have as a business owner. However, your accountant does not own or run your business. You do. Accountants serve in the role of consultants and advisors, not decision makers. You need to be able to evaluate the advice of your accountant (and all your other advisors) in the context of a global view of your business, your personal values and personal goals, and the ins and outs of making the many decisions you face.

We think hiring a business or office manager will solve the problem. Your business manager (if you decide to hire one) is an employee. He or she does not own or run the business and is likely not skilled at the level of decision making needed to run your business. Managing a business is quite different from leading it. Leading the business is your job. You establish the values of the business. You set the tone. You determine the vision, direction, and related policies and procedures (Walfish, Zimmerman, & Nordal, in press). Your business manager helps you implement what you would like to accomplish based on your vision. As an employee, your business manager also needs to be supervised. Without such supervision, a business or office manager can make decisions that are antithetical to your core values and even betray your trust (an all too frequent occurrence).

We don't acknowledge the right we have to take care of ourselves when it comes to running our business. Do you barely read and then sign a contract? Do you hire an associate without an employee agreement and simply pay what you guess others pay? Do you monitor your billing service? Do you avoid double-checking log sheets and deposit records? Does your office manager make all of your deposits for you? These are all, in our opinion, a form of business self-neglect that occurs when the owner of the practice does not truly engage in oversight behaviors that protect his or her business—*and personal*—interests. We strongly believe that you have an absolute right, even an obligation, to take a proactive approach in your business. You would expect it from others if you invested as much in their business as you've invested in yours. Have the same attitude about your own business.

The Importance of Understanding and Managing Your Finances

Understanding and managing your finances permeate almost every aspect of your practice, including the following:
- Signing a lease for office space
- Signing an agreement with an insurance carrier or managed care company
- Leasing or purchasing office equipment
- Hiring clinical and administrative staff
- Managing your tax obligations
- Securing a line of credit

- Securing insurance and other benefits for yourself and your employees
- Retirement savings and planning
- Furnishing your office
- Deciding on a billing service, software, or staff
- Deciding on compensation for staff
- Determining marketing initiatives
- Maximizing your returns on your investment (net profits and your compensation)
- Making sure you are getting paid for the services you and your clinical staff provide
- Minimizing theft (e.g., embezzlement)
- Deciding on continuing education
- Billing and collecting fees from clients

Sound financial management goes directly to your bottom line. Even minor shifts in management strategy make a major difference. For example, suppose George is a clinician who collects $100 an hour for 25 hours per week of direct service over 46 weeks of a calendar year (he doesn't work on legal holidays, and he also takes time off for vacations and continuing education). That adds up to a total of $115,000 of receivables into the practice. If his expenses are $34,500 (30%), he will net (or take home) $80,500 (before taxes).

However, if George can increase his revenue by just 5% (e.g., by reducing accounts receivable and bad debt and having a few more private pay instead of managed care clients), he would then earn $120,750 – $34,500 (overhead) = $86,250. This is tantamount to a pay raise of more than 7.75%.

If at the same time he reduced expenses by 5% (e.g., by restructuring his phone costs, subletting his office space part time, shifting the billing process to a more cost-effective system, decreasing marketing costs that are not producing positive returns), his overhead would then drop to $32,775. George's new net would then be $120,750 – $32,775 = $87,975. This is equivalent to a 9.3% raise without working any extra hours!

Let's take this one step further. Suppose George decided to dedicate just 2 more hours per week to seeing private pay patients, charging $150 per hour. That would bring in another $300 per week. Within 46 weeks, he would generate another $13,800, increasing his income to $101,775. This would be a gain of $21,275 (26.4%) over what he would have earned had he not made these relatively minor changes.

On the other hand, not being careful about your financial decisions can also negatively affect the bottom line. Deciding to contract with managed care carriers for rates that are heavily discounted (perhaps 50% off of your usual rate) will deeply cut into the amount of income you can generate. You may be able to work a few extra hours but most likely not enough to make up for the pay cut, not to mention how exhausted you'll be, which could have an impact on your effectiveness and increase the risk of clinical and ethical errors (Barnett et al., 2014).

A busy practice is not necessarily a profitable one. We have seen group practices lose money because their overhead (including staff compensation) is higher than the amount of money collected per session. How can this be? Costs of space, administrative staff, technology in the office, supplies, unemployment insurance, health insurance, workers compensation, and Social Security matching need to be taken into consideration in the cost of having personnel to deliver services. Unfortunately, if the practitioners are unaware that the fee structure they have set up isn't covering their costs and has resulted in their losing money each session, they may erroneously assume that bringing in more business will increase their bottom line. If their costs per visit increase over time, this would only further erode their profits, because it would cost them even more to provide the additional services.

This would be like your local store selling a product for $3.50 that cost them $5 to produce. Unless the storeowner can make up the loss some other way, she will eventually go out of business. Understanding these basic principles and looking at your figures can actually help you make informed business decisions (about what services to provide, how to set your fees, etc.). Without paying due diligence to the costs of doing business, it is difficult to determine how to develop and sustain a profitable enterprise.

A key strategy to make this work for you is simply to be attentive and actually look at what you are doing as if you were investing your own savings (because you are!). We suggest you take the position of saying, "I want to actively look after my own best interests." This can help you decide what to pay attention to. Especially pay attention to the finances related to the clinical services being delivered and the infrastructure that supports the service delivery (i.e., running the business). In so doing, a good habit (which we address in detail in Chapter 3) is to begin routinely collecting key data (called *metrics*) on your business. These are simple numbers to collect or compute, and they can tell you a great deal of information about your practice (Walfish et al., in press). These metrics are critical for making business decisions. We will show you how to look at some business decisions and analyze them from a financial perspective.

How It All Fits Together

You do not need to have a doctorate in economics, finance, or accounting to be able to apply basic principles and strategies of financial management to the business decisions about your practice. You do need to decide that your investment in your practice is important to manage with intention and that you are worth it. Once you make this shift, it is easy to start integrating this outlook into the myriad business decisions you face.

"Crunching the numbers" won't tell you everything you need to know, but it will help you get started in making informed decisions. Thinking about your practice as your personal $100,000+ investment can help you stay focused on taking care of it. Then making sure you have access to the necessary metrics, can really help you get a sense of how your investment is performing and where you might need to make changes or enhancements. The concepts in the chapters that follow are often foreign to the mental health professionals we meet. However, we've never met a clinician who could not grasp them. You can fear the unknown or embrace it. Join us in turning the unknown into the known and the fear into useful and profitable information.

two

Accounting and Finances 101

There are many financial terms used in the management of a practice with which a business owner or manager needs to become familiar. We start by defining some of this basic terminology and how the terms may relate to your practice. A glossary of terms is provided at the end of the book for your future reference.

Method of Accounting

There are two primary methods of accounting for a health care practice: the cash method of accounting and the accrual method of accounting. In most instances, health care practices use the cash basis of accounting for tax purposes. This accounting method allows a practice to report income as it is collected and deduct the expenses as they are paid.

The accrual basis of accounting requires you to record income when it is earned—that is, at the time of service—even though you may not receive payment for this service for days or months (e.g., payment from an insurance company; monthly payments from a contract to provide evaluations). On the expense side, you can take a deduction for an expense that you have incurred but not paid for as long as you are obligated for the purchase of the service or the product (e.g., legal services that have been rendered, but the practice has 30 days to pay the invoice; office supplies that are purchased on account and the practice does not have to pay for the supplies until the invoice is received).

From an accounting standpoint, the reason that most health care practices use the cash basis of accounting is due to the uncertainty of knowing what you will collect for your services. In many cases, you accept less than your actual billing under payer contracts with insurance companies. At times (hopefully not often), a client will not pay for the services that you provided. You would not want to pay income tax on the full amount of your billings or an estimated amount of billings when you will not likely collect that full amount.

General Ledger/Chart of Accounts

Your practice chart of accounts is a listing of all accounts (not bank accounts or check registers) that are relevant in describing your transaction (fees, rental income, payroll, utilities, etc.) and would be used in the posting of all of your transactions. These accounts fall into the following categories: assets, liabilities, equity, income, and expenses. These categories will be used in creating your financial reports that are described in this chapter. The assets, liabilities, and equity are recorded on what is called your *balance sheet*. The income and expenses will be recorded on your *profit and loss statement*. Your general ledger can be produced by your financial software. This report shows the detail of all transactions posted to each of your accounts. This is helpful for analyzing the breakout in any account so you will be able to see the detail of the transactions.

Balance Sheet

The balance sheet is the financial report that summarizes your practice's financial position. The balance sheet is broken down into three sections: assets, liabilities, and equity. In general, your assets will always equal the sum of your liabilities and your equity in the practice. To say it in a different way, your assets minus your liabilities will equal your equity in the practice. In other words, if you have $75,000 in assets (such as cash, equipment, and furnishings) and $20,000 in liabilities (such as loans), the equity of your practice would be $55,000. When examining the balance sheet, it can be somewhat confusing when you look at the *Total Assets* and then see the liability and equity section equal the total assets. You may think looking at the bottom line numbers that you business has greater value. In our example, the Total Assets line on the balance sheet would show $75,000. Instead, your eye should go to the *Total Equity* balance. That would be $55,000 ($75,000 total assets less $20,000 of liabilities) to determine the value you retain in the business for planning purposes. The report bottom line, which says *Total Liabilities and Equity*, is an accounting term that refers to the sum of the liabilities and equity and not the financial value of the business. The balance sheet tells the story of your financial viability, not your day-to-day cash flow.

Assets are property you own, both tangible and intangible. These assets are what your practice needs to run its operations. Examples of current and tangible assets would be cash in your bank and investment accounts, inventory, accounts receivable, furniture, fixtures, computer equipment, medical equipment, and software. Examples of intangible assets on the balance sheet are purchased goodwill (e.g., if you purchased another practice), loan fees, and costs of forming the practice.

Liabilities are debts the practice owes to others. These may include things such as bank debt, credit card debt, and amounts owed to vendors for items/services purchased, also known as accounts payable.

Your equity is the funds that you have actually invested in the business plus cumulative profits in the company that you have not withdrawn. Cumulative profits would be income earned in previous years that was not withdrawn from the business but have been used to reinvest in the business. On your balance sheet, these would be classified as retained earnings or owner's equity.

The balance sheet tells you as the business owner the financial strength of your business. If your assets are more than your liabilities, you are in a positive position. If you have more debts than assets, you are in a negative position. This means you would be using current income to pay prior debts. For example, if you have a large credit line balance and are paying that credit line down in the current year, you are using your current cash flow to pay past expenses. In a health care practice that is not highly equipment intensive, like a mental health practice as opposed to a dental practice, generally you would like your assets to be at least twice your liabilities to ensure adequate liquidity in your business. This is especially important if you experience a downturn in cash flow or need to make a significant investment in the practice. If your assets are two times your liabilities, you would know that you have the resources to pay off your debts and still have enough assets to secure your cash flow.

Profit and Loss Statement

The profit and loss statement provides the information regarding the current fiscal year profitability of the practice. The profit and loss statement starts with your income items, such as client fees, stipends, Employee Assistance Program fees, book royalties, speaking/workshop fees, and possibly rental income if you sublet part of your office space. Once you have the total income of the practice, you then need to concern yourself with your practice expenses. Your practice expenses are all of the payments you make to keep your practice running. Generally these expenses include, rent, cost of administrative staff, cost of clinician employees, office supplies, testing materials, dues and licenses, continuing education, insurance (including malpractice), and utilities, among others. The current year expenses do not include any loan principal payments when computing the net income for the year. Currently, only the interest portion of a loan payment would be deductible from your income. The net of the income and expenses is what you as the owner(s) of the practice have to compensate yourself for your time and financial investment assuming you do not have any debt. If you have debt, the funds that will be available for you to draw would be your net income less your principal loan payments. We use this report in Chapter 3 to help you learn how to analyze your practice as a whole and what should be important from this report to make effective decisions.

Budgets

Your practice's budget is a tool to help you reach your financial goals and objectives. This may seem like a daunting task or one that is not useful because you don't know exactly what your income or expenses will be for the year. It is neither. Think of your budget as your road map to the next year. It will not be perfect, and there will be detours along the way, but during the year it will allow you to analyze where the detours are and how to fix or go around them or to reassess spending decisions. Your budget is the measurement you use each month to determine whether you are on track to meet your financial goals. Most accounting software can generate a budget report showing what your actual income and expenses were compared with what you budgeted them to be.

For example, suppose your budget has you being compensated $100,000 for the year, and you base your personal spending on this projection. It's important to look at your actual income frequently to make sure that you are on track and to make adjustments if not. The earlier in the year that you do this, the less likely that you will reach the end of the year with insufficient money to pay your bills.

The budget should create productivity goals for yourself and your clinicians if you are in a group practice. On the income side, it mostly relates to billable hours and collections, although other sources of income, including rent collected, should be included as well. This is the starting point to your budget.

Once you have your income budget set from these goals, you can then work on projecting your expenses. Many of your expenses are fixed monthly expenses that you have little discretion over, such as rent, utilities, telephone, and insurance. These expenses are the easiest to budget because the costs are relatively fixed. The variable expense that can change based on productivity or management decisions are a bit harder to budget. Based on the current income projections, what level of administrative staff do you need? Are you starting new programs that require start-up costs? How can you control office supply costs? These are just a few of the factors to consider.

In addition to these expenses, it is also important to keep a capital (or major) expenditure budget for items such as computers, office improvements, and electronic health records systems. Whether we like it or not, things break, computer systems become outdated, and new psychological tests are developed. It is good to get your practice into a cycle of periodically replacing computers or other items that need updating every few years. If you budget each year for one or two computers, it is easier to handle this in a given year compared with trying to project for a budget in which you are purchasing five or six big-ticket items in one year. If you consistently budget for ongoing upgrades, it is less likely that you will be caught with a large unexpected cost.

Once you have the budget put together, the net will be the owner profit or compensation. Is this the number you anticipated? If it is lower, you will need to go back to the assumptions in the budget to determine ways to increase revenue or decrease expenses.

You should review the completed budget against the last 2 years of actual results. How is it different? How is it similar? What are the reasons for the differences? Have you created an achievable budget, or one that is set up for failure? A budget needs to be realistic and achievable for it be an effective management tool. If you spend the entire year chasing a budget that was so overreaching from the beginning, your will experience a lot of stress and likely be viewing your net earnings as not measuring up to your expectations (that were unrealistically high in the first place).

When creating budgets, we believe a conservative approach that results in a reasonable compensation to the owners is better than a budget that creates an overly optimistic expectation of the owners and then does not reach the expectation. It is better to beat the expectation because this helps you stay motivated (and can give you a pleasant bonus at the end of the year).

On the other hand, don't aim too low. First, low expectations can keep you from reaching your potential. Second, it doesn't make sense to struggle with a highly restrictive budget that stresses you for 11 months, only to enjoy a large bonus at the end of the year. It may also have you earning less than a reasonable amount from the practice throughout the year and hence cause you to be stressed regarding personal finances for most of the year.

Generally, it is a good practice to slightly underestimate income and overestimate expenses. For example, be sure not to budget 52 weeks of income (as clinicians take vacations, there are holidays, weather-related closures of the practice, and other days off that are unpredictable). Also, be sure to remember to budget unpredictable expenses (such as computer maintenance, equipment that needs to be replaced, increases in insurance premiums that may not be known when you construct the budget).

Accounts Payable

Accounts payable are amounts that are due to your vendors. These are bills that have come in for products or services received that you have not yet paid (e.g., utility bills and charges from your billing service). In a business with good cash flow, most of the accounts payable are paid within 30 days to maintain good credit with your vendors. If your vendor offers an early pay discount for paying within 10 days, consider taking advantage of that offer. The money you save goes directly to the bottom line and ideally your wallet. Looking at the accounts payable report helps you know how well your current bank balance represents the money you actually will have available after you pay your outstanding bills. If you have $10,000 in your bank account and also have $2,000 in accounts payable, then you should regard it as having only $8,000 of cash on hand. Similarly, if you have $15,000 in your bank account and $10,000 accounts payable, that is essentially equivalent to having only $5,000 cash on hand.

Accounts Receivable

Accounts receivable is the money that clients, insurance companies, or any other group you have done work for owe to you for the rendering of professional services. In most cases you should monitor this by the age of the accounts receivable—that is, the length of time between your bill being sent and when you receive payment. Most of your accounts receivable should be collected within 60 days of billing for that service. Any items that are greater than 30 days old require your attention because the longer you wait, the more difficult it gets to actually collect what is due. When reviewing your receivables, ask yourself:

- Are there insurance claims that need to be resubmitted due to (a) a denial of the initial claim or (b) their statement to you that the claim was never received?
- Are you still providing services to self-pay patients that owe you for past services, but not discussing with them how they can put a payment plan in place?
- Are your claims being submitted in a timely fashion?

Monitoring your accounts receivable is an absolutely essential task that you, as a business owner, need to stay on top of each month. Your billings and collections staff (or service) should be printing an aged accounts receivable report for you at the end of each month. If you do your own billing and use a software program (e.g., TherapyNotes; Therapist Helper), you can generate this type of report. The report will show you the outstanding amounts to be collected for services billed and how long the charge has been outstanding. Typically you will see the categories on this report as current, or overdue by 30 days, 60 days, 90 days, and more than 120 days. You should be reviewing the monthly aged list with your administrative person that is responsible for your billing and collections. If you have clinical staff working for you, you may need to sit with the professionals who have accounts with aged collections and review them. If you do not take the outstanding balances seriously, it is unlikely your staff and clients will.

It is important that clinical staff members in a group practice review these reports closely and be actively involved in the billing and collections process. There are a few reasons for this. First, if they are compensated on the basis of a percentage of collections received, then it is in their best interest to optimize the fees collected from clients. Second, clinicians place themselves at ethical risk when they have poor collection practices (Barnett & Walfish, 2010; Barnett, Zimmerman, & Walfish, 2014). Insurers require that reasonable attempts be made to collect copays due. Except in occasional hardship situations, Medicare may consider it fraud not to collect copays from its beneficiaries. Third, nonpayment of fees can sometimes be a financial issue, but more often than not, it is a clinical issue that should be addressed with clients. Do they not value your services? Are they angry at you? Do they not feel obligated to keep to financial agreements that they made? Are they narcissistic and feel entitled to free health care? For these reasons, in a group practice it is essential that clinicians not simply defer all financial issues to "the business office."

Debts: Loans and Lines of Credit

The financial health of your practice is also affected by the amount of debt and the monthly costs of carrying or paying the interest on the debt. This can be debt acquired along the way and also from the start-up of your practice. Practices are initially funded in many different ways. In some cases, the owner(s) contributes the cash for the start-up expenses such as rent, utilities, and administration cost until the first client/insurance checks start to come in. He or she then continues to invest in the practice by not taking any funds personally until the company gets to the position of having more income each month then expenses. Some practices borrow money from a bank to obtain the start-up cash need and plan to pay the loan back over a 5- or 7-year period. These loans in today's banking world are harder to get approved because the practice itself has little equity or collateral for the bank to secure the note. Banks may be more willing to make the loan if you have personal collateral with which you can secure the loan as a guarantee.

Once the practice is established and has assets, accounts receivable, and a history of financial records showing a positive cash flow, it is advisable to seek a line of credit from a bank. This will provide you with some sense of security should your cash flow slow down for some reason (e.g., insurance companies holding back payments; a downturn in business). A credit line allows you to draw down on the note to meet immediate cash flow needs. You then pay it back with interest once your cash flow crunch is resolved. The rule of thumb is to have a line of credit for approximately 2 to 3 months of operating expenses. It is important to be regimented in paying the loan back quickly so that it does not become just another outstanding debt that decreases the equity of the practice.

In some cases practices have other debts as a result of purchasing equipment, furniture, or technology to run the practice. These are typically term loans that are repaid at a fixed rate of interest over a set period of time, such as 36, 48, or 60 months. Although any practice would prefer to be debt-free, sometimes larger expenses (e.g., moving to a larger office; purchasing specialized software or buying other expensive equipment) need to be supported by debt to keep the practice functioning in an efficient manner. When you are considering a major expenditure, your sources to pay for the purchase would be from current cash flow or by borrowing the funds, or a combination of the two. If you use significant cash flow from any one year to make the purchase, that will decrease your available partner (owner) income in that year and may not allow you to take the cash flow you need from the practice for your own personal finances and security. As part of the budgeting process, you should consider future capital expenditures that may be needed in the practice and decide how those will be paid. Please see Chapter 4 for more information on loans and leases.

Setting Up Your Practice Management and Accounting Systems

It is imperative to have a good accounting system and a practice management system to be able to access data that can help you effectively manage your practice. Your practice's financial books and records should be separate from your personal accounts. You should have a separate bank account and accounting system for your practice. This separation is extremely important for many reasons, but the most important reason is that it will keep the Internal Revenue Service from examining all of your personal information if your practice were to be audited. If the financial books and records are comingled, you will need to open up all of your information for them to review.

The financial accounting system and the practice management system are usually separate software products. A software package that does both is typically very expensive. Many health care practices use accounting software such as QuickBooks to maintain their accounting books and records. This software allows you to record deposits and pay bills and provides you with financial reports (monthly, quarterly, or yearly) based on the data you input to help you analyze the financial status of your business. On a monthly basis, you should at minimum run the following reports: (1) balance sheet, (2) profit and loss statement, and (3) budget to actual report showing variances of actual income and expense from your budgeted or projected figures.

If you have associates, in many cases you will want to set up what are called *classes* in your accounting system so that you can record income received, payroll, and direct expenses for each clinician. This provides you the ability to review the contribution/cost of each associate to determine his or her contribution to the general overhead of the practice and the profit/loss of the practice. It will also allow you to compare them (or different clinical programs) to one another from a financial and profit perspective.

The initial design of any accounting software requires some thought and discussion with your financial advisor to highlight key data that you would like to retrieve easily from the system. Up-front work on the setup may spare you the time later to change the settings of the system after data have already been entered. Although the configuration of the software can be changed down the road, it is far preferable to have some clear and concise thoughts about your needs right from the outset.

Choosing Your Accountant

When choosing an accountant for your practice, the best place to start is to ask your friends and colleagues in business for recommendations. If you can get two to three referrals, you can interview the potential candidates. The person you choose should have experience with other mental health practices. Ask for references and check them. Ask the references how quickly the accountant responds to phone calls and e-mails. Once you have narrowed the field, you should think about who you felt most comfortable with. Your accountant should be your "go-to" person when you have a financial practice issue or question. You should choose someone you will feel comfortable reaching out to when you have a question. The positive relationship you develop with your accountant will enhance your practice because you will feel comfortable reaching out for both your strategic practice issues as well as routine day-to-day questions.

How It All Fits Together

It is important to use the tools we've discussed in this chapter so that the practice does not manage you, but you manage the practice with well-thought-out decisions based on current facts and figures that you can rely on. There is a saying in the accounting world: "Junk in equals junk out." You and your accountant need to be able to rely fully on the information produced by your software. Therefore, it is critical that the person responsible for the day-to-day input into the system understands the needs of the practice and how each piece relates to the whole picture. You need someone who will watch out for the best interest of the practice. This is a key role in your practice, and you should not minimize the time and skill level of the person needed to do this work. Think carefully about whom you will entrust with this important function.

three

Practice Metrics

To assess the health or wellness of any system, we look at the degree of change across key elements over a period of time. Your dentist and doctors take multiple, repeated measurements related to your physical health. Economists examine specific measures as they try to determine the fiscal health of our country or a particular segment of the economy. Individual businesses—from Fortune 500 companies to your local small businesses—do this routinely and then set performance standards and goals related to these elements. For example, a donut shop may track how fast its customers get served. A customer service center may count how many rings it takes until someone answers the phone. A manufacturer may determine the cost of producing one widget or 10 or 20 different widgets. All of these types of data are vital pieces of information that help the business owners estimate the potential profits associated with the product or service they are providing, thereby guiding many related business decisions.

Tracking key business metrics is necessary to successfully run a mental health practice. Whether you are in a solo practice, office-sharing practice, or group practice, you need to be able to take the equivalent of your business' pulse and blood pressure. Otherwise, you could make important, even crucial, business decisions blindly, just by your "sense" of how things are going. Is this is how you would want a company you have invested in (or your doctor) to make key decisions that could affect your future?

In this chapter, we present some key measures that we believe are important to keep track of on a regular basis. You, of course, can decide which ones you want to track now and perhaps which you will track later (or not at all). None of these metrics require complex math skills. Additionally, none require sophisticated and expensive software. You can probably calculate them from a combination of whatever software programs and administrative services (e.g., your billing service, bookkeeper, office manager, accountant) you already have in place. In the following pages, we walk you through the basic metrics and then show you how to succinctly summarize them. We also show you how you can drill deeper into the figures to find out even more about your business. Last, we will show you how it all fits together.

Key Metrics

There are four main categories of business information for you to consider: (1) income and expenses, (2) billing and production, (3) collections and accounts receivable, and (4) referrals and origination of work. These four categories of information will give you a head start into understanding what is happening in your practice from a business perspective. You can use this information to help guide you in making decisions that are aligned with the vision of your practice, the allocation of your financial resources, and your tolerance for financial risk.

As we describe each of these four areas, we present some of the key metrics, suggest where you can get the information, and show you what you can learn from the data. We use information from a hypothetical practice and generally keep the numbers as rounded estimates. Rather than focusing on the actual specific numerical amount and how it compares to your practice, we would rather you focus on the concepts and how the metrics fit together to tell a story about this sample practice. You do not need a calculator. We will even take care of the math and show you just how simple it is to calculate the figures that will give you a good sense of many aspects of your practice.

Income and Expenses

The profit and loss (P&L) statement (Chapter 2) that comes from your accountant (or that you generate) will show the total income collected over the course of a reporting year (often a calendar year).

Typically, most of this income will be from professional fees and stipends. However, as we mentioned in Chapter 2, there may be other sources of income such as royalties (if you have authored books) and rental income (if you sublease your office). It is important to keep track of these different sources of income because your practice analyses will center on what you collected from the professional services rendered. For example, let's say that the practice actually collected $300,000 over the course of the year.

Next, let's look at the expenses of the practice. Again, this information will be on the P&L. It will usually be quite detailed regarding the types of expenses. While the IRS may need all this detail (and you might find it interesting as well), for the sake of this exercise, we are only going to look at three kinds of expenses: compensation to clinical staff (not including compensation you personally take from the practice), compensation to administrative staff, and the total of your other office expenses or overhead. In our example, the expenses total $200,000 ($86,750 paid to clinical staff, $50,000 paid to administrative staff, and $63,250 for other office overhead expenses).

This leaves a net or profit of $100,000 ($300,000 income – $200,000 of total expenses) to the owner or owners (that's you). This number will also be on your P&L and is often referred to as the *bottom line*. Tracking this number quarterly or annually can give you an indication of whether you are making more or less money each year from the practice and whether, over multiple years, there are predictable cyclical changes. In short, these figures tell you how much return you are earning from your investment of money, time, and energy into your practice.

These figures also give you the ability, when combined with some other rather simple metrics, to obtain important information about your practice. For example, if we simply divide the amount of expenses or overhead ($200,000) by the amount collected ($300,000), we get an overhead ratio of 67%, which means that 33% goes to the owner(s). Of course, that is not equivalent to 33% profit because the owner(s) of a mental health practice also likely provided clinical services that contribute to the total collected. Therefore, the 33% also compensates the owners for the professional services they rendered.

Perhaps a more useful metric is the overhead that does not include the clinician compensation, as follows:

Part-time administrative staff: $50,000
Other expenses: $63,250
Total administrative expenses: $113,250
Total collected: $300,000
Total administrative expenses / total collected: 38%

This shows us that 38% of the professional fees collected goes to running the practice (paying for administrative staff, other services, insurance, rent, etc.).

In our view, this figure, which we call the *administrative overhead ratio*, is a basic element of key practice decisions. First, it can give you a sense of how the expenses are tracking compared with the income produced. For example, if next year the practice expanded and its income was at $400,000 (an increase of $100,000 or 33%) and the nonprofessional overhead was $160,000, the administrative overhead ratio would be 40%, indicating that more of every dollar was going to keep the practice running and that actually the owners are making less per dollar earned, even though the practice is earning more dollars! In other words, it is now costing more per dollar to actually run the practice. In business terms the average *margin*, or profit from each dollar earned (or unit of service provided), is actually less, even though the practice's overall revenue greatly increased. This is an important computation that can help you gauge whether expansion is a good idea. Sometimes, long-term forecasting can predict that the total profits generated may make up for a decrease in the net generated per unit of service. Other times, you may find that the risk of losing money is just too great to justify the expansion.

We can use the administrative overhead ratio to show how (as in the example in Chapter 1) a practice can actually lose money with every unit of service provided. Let's look at your practice clinicians and imagine that the clinicians in the practice get paid an average of 50% of what they collect. When we add to that the 38% overhead, we have a total of 88% of what is collected going to the clinicians, other staff, and other expenses, leaving 12% for the owner(s). When the administrative ratio is now 40%, as in the second instance, that makes the total overhead 90%, leaving only 10% of the clinicians' net income for the owner. Now imagine that in the following year, the same practice decides to pay its clinicians 55% of what they generate as an incentive, and the administrative overhead ratio increases by another 5% to 43%, totaling 98%. The 10% margin or profit drops to only 2%. At this point, the owners are just about at a break-even point on the clinicians' net income. If the profit reduces much more, they will be losing money each time a clinician provides a service (however, you need to factor in that the clinicians' income is still being used to offset some of the practice's expenses).

Second, the administrative overhead ratio can be a signal to closely analyze the specific expenses that the practice is paying. What we have found is that simple and small shifts in the expenses can go a long way to providing income to the owner without sacrificing the quality of the office, services provided, or employee relations. For example, negotiating lower phone rates by $30 per month ($360/year), loan rates on a line of credit by $50 per month ($600/year), and reducing rent by $100 per month ($1,200/year) can all lead to major changes to the bottom line (in this case, $180/month or $2,160/year). Subleasing an office to effectively decrease your overall rental exposure can also have the same impact. In fact, we find that when practices simply make a 5% reduction in their expenses, the take-home compensation of the owner(s) can increase by thousands of dollars per year, and much more when this savings is accrued over the next 5 to 10 years.

One other useful metric in this category is to examine the income and expense figures as they relate to the number of visits provided over the same time period. In our example, the practice provided a total of 2,500 visits. They collected $120 per visit ($300,000 collected / 2,500 visits). Their average expense per visit was $80 ($200,000 expenses / 2,500 visits) with a net profit of $40 per visit ($120 collected – $80 expenses). Remember, however, that this "profit" figure of $40 per visit also goes to compensate you for your clinical work because the owner's production of revenue to the practice is included in the amount collected (i.e., the $300,000).

This profit-per-visit figure can be especially important when comparing different types of services that you provide or are considering providing. For example, suppose you are thinking of increasing your substance abuse services, hiring a neurofeedback technician, or joining another managed care provider group.

To arrive at a profit-per-visit figure, you would first estimate what you would generate per visit. Then subtract the anticipated compensation to the professional providing the service and also subtract your nonsalary overhead. Do this for each of the various services you are considering, and compare them to one another and the overall profits of the practice, to see what might make sense from a financial perspective.

Let's look at how that would play out in our example. *We make the assumption that overhead costs would incrementally increase at the same rate per visit for new service lines.* However, when doing the full analysis for an added service line, you would need to project both the additional income to the practice as well as the additional or incremental expenses for an accurate analysis. The practice at large brings in $120 per visit and has $45.60 (38%) of administrative overhead expenses per visit. This leaves $74.40 available to pay professional compensation and for net profit. Now, let's look at the other three options.

The substance abuse evaluation contract is at $900 per evaluation. You expect each evaluation to take about 5 hours of professional time (records review, face-to-face evaluation, report scoring and writing, etc.). The clinician will make 50% ($450) leaving $450 to the practice. At 5 hours we would expect $228 ($45.60/hour) to go toward administrative expenses, leaving $222 (or $44.40/hour) to go to the bottom line or profits of the practice.

The neurofeedback technician will charge $95 an hour and be paid $47.50 an hour. However, do we expect that the office overhead will go down, or will it stay the same from a dollars-and-cents perspective? It is important to think about this carefully. The rent, malpractice insurance, secretarial salary, and so on do not decrease simply because the revenue per hour decreases. So when we look at the $95 per hour of revenue and subtract the $47.50 per hour the technician is being paid and the $45.60 per hour of office overhead, we find that this service is barely breaking even ($95 – $47.50 – $45.60 = $1.90). If the calculations (e.g., as a result of overestimating productivity, underestimating expenses, or 100% of fees not being collected) are off a bit, this service could easily lose money. There would need to be another compelling reason, from a business standpoint, to add this service (e.g., having the expectation of collateral referrals or dramatically reducing expenses by offering the service in a physician's office at a far reduced rent) to the practice.

Finally, if we look at the managed care contract that is paying $75 an hour, we find that we would pay the clinical staff $37.50 an hour (i.e., 50% of $75). Our administrative overhead would still be $45.60. Adding the two together, we would be bringing in $75 per hour and having $83.10 per hour of costs ($37.50 to the clinician and $45.60 for other administrative overhead). In other words, we would be losing $8.10 an hour to provide the services in this particular contract (presuming the actual administrative expenses to manage the contract did increase by the same overhead percentage).

Now, before you make a quick decision here, there might actually be a circumstance when you might take the managed care contract. You might consider signing the contract if you were certain that there would be another more lucrative stream of income generated as a result (e.g., the physicians who refer the managed care patients to you are also referring patients for substance abuse evaluations or non–managed care fee-for-service full-fee patients). Additionally, you might decide to take on a new revenue line if your analysis showed that your overhead costs would not increase on a per-visit basis at the same rate. For example, some new product lines (such as groups or specialized treatment programs) might not generate many incremental costs. A new source of revenue with no increase to overhead would actually decrease the overall overhead percentage.

You should carefully think through these types of decisions. There should be a clear advantage to pursuing one line of service delivery with more vigor than the others.

Billings and Collections

Unfortunately, some key metrics are not included in your typical P&L. These are the total amount billed and the total amount adjusted against that billed amount. Fortunately, these numbers should be easy to gather from your billing software or service.

In our practice example, we are going to assume that the practice collectively billed $400,000 and also adjusted out or wrote off $100,000 that was not collected (mostly as a result of the discounts given to the managed care contracts). We have found that a useful figure to track over time is the ratio of what was collected ($300,000) to what was billed ($400,000), or 75%. This is an important number (we call it the *collection ratio*) because it can help you assess whether the practice is collecting more or less of what it bills over time. If you are building a niche practice or changing some of your participation in managed care contracts, this metric can show you some of the impact of those changes. We look at it as a statement of how successfully the practice is collecting what it bills; the higher the percentage the better. A practice that is fully out of managed care and has a low accounts receivable would generally have a collection ratio of more than 90%. A practice that is almost fully dependent on managed care could easily have a collection ratio of about 50% because it might only collect about half of what it bills. Thus, when looking at your collection ratio, it is important to take into account your payer sources. Alternatively, you can use a collection ratio that is based on your actual collections divided by your expected collections. This can be particularly helpful for practices that are heavily into managed care or other contracts in which they accept a fee that is quite lower than their usual and customary fee.

Let's look at what happens if we consider the billings and collections as they relate to the number of clinicians. If this practice has a total of 2.5 full-time clinicians (including the owner), we find that the average billed per full-time clinician is $160,000 ($400,000 billed / 2.5 clinicians) and the average collected is $120,000 per clinician ($300,000 collected / 2.5 clinicians). Let's say you are considering yourself as having a full-time clinical load (i.e., generating $120,000 of income into the practice). We also saw in the previous section on profits and losses that there was $100,000 available after we took all the income ($300,000) and subtracted from it all of the expenses ($200,000). Thus, overall you personally made $100,000 of compensation and generated $120,000 of income. In other words you made 83.3% of what you brought in! Your personal overhead was 16.7%. That is quite different from what your employees are making (50% of what they collect). This difference is one thing that compensates you for taking the financial risks you have taken, building the practice, running the practice, and dealing with all the business decisions and negotiations to which you attend.

Next we translate the billings and collections figures into per visit metrics. We can see that the practice is billing $160 per visit ($400,000 billed / 2,500 visits) and as we know from earlier in the chapter, the practice is collecting $120 per visit. We also can see that the average number of visits per clinician is 1,000 (2,500 visits / 2.5 clinicians). To gauge of overall productivity (hours generating revenue), divide 1,000 hours by 46 weeks (reducing the usual 52 weeks by holidays, vacations, sick, and other days off). The resulting figure shows that the average full-time clinician bills 21.7 hours per week or 4.3 hours per day (21.7 hr / 5 workdays).

If you wanted to increase your profit, one initiative might be to explore how your average clinician could increase billable time per day. Adding just 2 more billable hours a day per full-time clinician would generate a total of 5 hours more per day (25 hours more per week) of billable time for the practice at large. Over the course of your 46-week year, this would create 1,150 more billable hours at $120 per visit or $138,000 more revenue into the practice! It's almost like having another full-time clinician billing without needing to hire someone.

Of course, part of that extra income will be paid out as compensation to the clinicians. However, if 50% of what was generated went to compensate the clinicians, that would still leave $69,000 toward the bottom line, assuming (as we did earlier) that your fixed administrative expenses would not substantially change (except perhaps for payroll taxes and the incremental expenses associated with billing, collections, and supplies). These kinds of forward-thinking projections, and use of the metrics, help make it clear that an important practice initiative is to increase the productivity of your clinical staff. The difference between 4.3 hours per day and 6.3 hours per day of productivity is huge.

You could even use this analysis to design an incentive program that you might otherwise not have previously considered. While many practice owners simply announce that everyone needs to be more productive, you might decide to dedicate a bit of that $69,000 (let's say 10%, or almost $7,000) as an incentive to the clinicians who make a substantial increase (you would need to define this in advance) in their productivity and collections. That is, in addition to their 50% of what they bring in, you might decide to offer them an additional bonus (either percentage or flat amount) for reaching additional collections targets that presumably would be achieved by increasing their billing as well. Walfish and Barnett (2009) describe a *floating percentage* model in which there are financial incentives for clinicians to see more clients. Which practice would you rather work for, the one with or without the incentive bonus? Which practice would you rather invest in or own?

Accounts Receivable

Your billing software, system, or service should provide your accounts receivable figures on a monthly basis. As we mentioned, this information is usually presented as a total and then broken down by the number of months the receivable has been outstanding. This set of data is rich with information.

In our sample practice the accounts receivable reads as follows:

0–30 days—$4,500
31–60 days—$3,500
61–90 days—$2,000
91–120 days—$4,000
120 days—$5,000
Total outstanding: $19,000

Putting aside what later would be adjusted out due to managed care contracted rates, we can see that there is less outstanding money 1 or 2 months out compared with the current month (0–30 days). This seems positive and in the right direction at first glance because you want to be collecting more of the billing sooner and not have it add to your aged accounts receivables. However, if we look to 3 and 4+ months out, we see that almost half ($9,000) of all the outstanding money ($19,000) is still outstanding. It is worth taking note of this, as it could signify some of the account balances that are 31–90 days aged will later "spill over" into the 91–120+ days categories as time marches on. In some respects, accounts that aged are like fruit. The longer they are on the vine, the more apt they are to spoil. In other words, the longer the debt is outstanding, the less likely it is to be collected.

Accounts should generally be collected within 60 days, with only a small amount of money going uncollected. In the above example, approximately half of what is uncollected goes missing from the practice (the balance is clinician compensation) and is then missing directly from the bottom line. Improving collections can improve cash flow and profitability. It can also help you avoid dealing with collection agencies, small claims court, and possibly licensure boards (Barnett, Zimmerman, & Walfish, 2014).

Case Origination

So far, we have looked at metrics related to the flow of cash in and out of the practice. Now we shift gears to focus on the sources of your income. A viable practice needs to have a reasonable flow of referrals, so that new cases help replace the attrition in cash flow when cases are completed or when clients leave the practice. Knowing where your clientele is coming from can help guide your marketing and staff development activities.

In our practice example, there have been 100 new cases. If we divide this by the total number of full-time clinicians (2.5), we see that there are on average 40 new cases per clinician per year, or less than 1 new case per week. If we think about the workload or productivity that we spoke about in the Billings and Collections section, we can start to see a picture taking shape here as it relates to productivity.

Let's think about how many referrals someone may need to stay "full." If the practice determines that to meet its budgeted income goals, each full time clinician is expected to bill 30 visits (or hours) per week for 46 weeks a year, this means there needs to be a total of 1,380 billable hours per clinician per year (46 × 30). Practice-wide, there would need to be a total of 3,450 (1380 × 2.5) billable hours over the course of the year. However, in our example, there were only 2,500 hours of billable time, or 72.5% of what is needed. Said another way, the 100 referrals only provided 72.5% of the needed level of production. There would have needed to be 138 referrals (100 / .725) for the expected level of production to be met given the current average number of sessions per case. It might also be useful to examine whether some clinicians are having cases prematurely terminate treatment, as this would lower the average number of visits per referral.

To gauge the impact of this difference, one can roughly estimate that the practice is grossing (before salaries and other expenses) $3,000 per new case ($300,000 income / 100 new cases). This, of course, is a rough estimate because it does not address the revenue generated from long-term cases. If the practice saw 38 more cases (138 budgeted – 100 actual), it would equate to $114,000 more gross income! If approximately 50% goes to clinician salaries, that leaves $57,000 to cover extra administrative staff time and payroll taxes, with the rest going directly to profits. Conservatively, you as the owner could get a raise of more than $40,000. Your clinicians would also make more money.

If you were thinking about your business plan for the coming year, based on the foregoing information, you might think of two initiatives. First, consider incentivizing your clinicians to work harder (perhaps giving a discretionary bonus if they surpass their targets by a certain amount). Second, you might decide to invest in marketing efforts to boost referrals. But where do you start in targeting your marketing initiatives?

Again, the answer can be found in your practice metrics. If you have tracked your new cases by referral partner (Walfish, Zimmerman, & Nordal, in press), you can determine where the gaps are as well as your most lucrative referral partners (i.e., the best paying sources of revenue). In some cases, these referral partners might not be those who send you the most clients. They may be those who send you more full-fee clients. You should carefully examine the workload related to each referral partner to see who are your best. For example, when looking at the referral data, let's say that physicians have referred you 70 of the 100 clients, and virtually all of those are covered by managed care. This would mean that 70% (70 of 100) of your services are sold at a steeply discounted contracted managed care rate (perhaps about half of your customary fee, or what would be called "wholesale" if you were selling a retail product). On the other hand, if previous clients ("word of mouth"), Internet marketing, and attorneys have generally brought in self-pay patients (30 new cases combined this past year), you might determine that these sources of revenue are worth pursuing even more vigorously because the anticipated revenue would likely be at least double per hour of service. In other words, it would take twice as many physician-referred managed care cases to generate approximately the same revenue as would be obtained from these other referral partners! As you can see, a few simple computations can point you in the direction of whether you should prioritize your marketing dollars and energies into developing relationships with physicians or focus more on (1) developing relationships with attorneys and (2) building your Internet marketing. You might also note that not all managed care contracts are equal: Some may reimburse at rates 30% to 40% higher than the lowest paying ones. If the higher paying carriers can be identified, then perhaps efforts can be made to attract clients with this insurance rather than those who pay the significantly lower amounts.

Additionally, you might run an outcome study of sorts to see how your current clients value the services you provide. On the basis of their responses, you can plan ways to increase the overall level of client satisfaction (which will presumably motivate them to mention you to their friends and extended family). For example, psychologist Keely Kolmes has developed a questionnaire to routinely collect client satisfaction data. She then presents this data on her website for potential clients and referral partners to review. This valuable feedback can let clinicians know how they are doing from the perspective of their clients, rather than overestimate their own skill level and outcome success, which is a result of self-assessment bias (Walfish, McAllister, O'Connell, & Lambert, 2012). Information about Dr. Kolmes's measure may be found at http://drkkolmes.com/client-satisfaction.

How It All Fits Together

Using the sample metrics reviewed in this chapter, you can set realistic and relevant practice initiatives, and then track your progress monthly, quarterly, or annually. A convenient way to view several key metrics all at once at a given point in time is via a "dashboard," as shown in Figure 3.1.

Figure 3.1 Dashboard

Line #	INCOME AND EXPENSES		BILLINGS AND COLLECTIONS		ACCOUNTS RECEIVABLE		
1	Total Collected	$300,000	Total Billed	$400,000		Dollars	Percent
2	Total Expenses (not including owner's compensation)	$200,000	Total Adjusted	$100,000	0-30 Days	$4,500	24%
3	Total Compensation to Professional Staff	$86,750	Total Collected	$300,000	31-60 Days	$3,500	18%
4	Total Compensation to Administrative Staff	$50,000	Collection Ratio (3/1)	75%	61-90 Days	$2,000	11%
5	Other Office Overhead Expenses	$63,250	Write-off Ratio (2/1)	25%	91-120 Days	$4,000	21%
6	Net (1-2)	$100,000			>120 Days	$5,000	26%
7	Overhead Ratio (2/1)	67%	Number of Clinicians (Including owner)	2.50	Total	$19,000	100%
8	Administrativel Overhead (4+5)/(1)	38%	Average Billed per Clinician (1/7)	$160,000			
9			Average Collected per Clinicain (3/7)	$120,000			
10							
11	**By Visit**		**By Visit**		**CASE ORIGINATION**		
12	Total # of visits	2500	Total # of visits	2500	Number of New Cases	100	
13	Average Collected per Visit (1/12)	$120	Average Billed per Visit (1/12)	$160	Number of Clinicians	2.50	
14	Average Expenses per Visit (2/12)	$80	Average Collected per Visit (3/12)	$120	Average Number of New Cases per Clinician (1/2)	40	
15	Net per Visit (13-14)	$40	Average Visits per Clincian (12/7)	1000	Total Collected	$300,000	
16					Average Collected per Case (4/1)	$3,000	

Figure 3.1 shows all of the metrics we have just reviewed on one page. You can use such a dashboard on a regular basis to take the pulse of your practice.

Annual Comparisons

Now we are going to take it two steps further. First we'll zoom out and compare these figures to those of the last 3 years. Then, we'll zoom in to see what is happening with the different clinicians. There are, of course, many other ways you can look at the data (e.g., by quarter, diagnosis, CPT code, insurer, etc.). We have decided, in this case, to examine only the clinician data.

Figure 3.2 Performance by Year

OVERALL INFO	FY1	FY2	FY3	FY4
Total Billed	$150,000	$225,000	$320,000	$400,000
Total Collected	$112,000	$185,000	$260,000	$300,000
Collection Ratio	75%	82%	81%	75%
Total Adjusted	$40,000	$60,000	$80,000	$100,000
Adjustment Ratio	27%	27%	25%	25%
Compensation to Professional Staff	$0	$40,000	$70,000	$86,750
Other Overhead (Admin staff + other expenses)	$45,000	$60,000	$75,000	$113,250
Total Overhead (Expenses)	$45,000	$100,000	$145,000	$200,000
Net	$67,000	$85,000	$115,000	$100,000
Overhead Ratio	40%	54%	56%	67%
Administrative Overhead Ratio	40%	32%	29%	38%
Profit Ratio	60%	46%	44%	33%
VISIT INFO				
Number of Visits	1000	1500	2000	2500
$ Billed/Visit	$150	$150	$160	$160
$ Collected/Visit	$112	$123	$130	$120
Expenses/Visit	$45	$67	$73	$80
Net/Visit	$67	$57	$58	$40
Number of Full-time Equivalent Clinicians	1.00	1.50	2.00	2.50
Visits/Full-time Clinician	1000	1000	1000	1000

The data we have already reviewed are summarized in the column labeled FY4 (Fiscal Year 4). To the left of that column are the annual data for the 3 prior years. At first glance, moving down the first two rows of data, you can see that the practice has more than doubled the amount billed and the amount collected. This is encouraging, and if you looked at just these first two rows you might think, "We're doing pretty well. Look at all the growth we have achieved." However, that's only part of the story. As we continue to look at the other statistics, we can see that in FY2 and FY3, the practice was actually collecting more of what it billed (greater than 80%), but this has dropped off again in FY4 and is now back at 75%. We can also see a bit of decline in the percent adjusted. This may mean there is more money collected, or it may mean that there is a bit of an increase in non–managed care revenue. This would require further analysis to sort out. We can also see that more money is being paid to the professional staff and to administrative overhead. All of this is to be expected as a practice grows. However, if you examine the line labeled "Net," you can see that there was actually $15,000 less available to the owner in FY4 than in FY3. Continuing to read down the table, you'll notice that in FY4, the ratio of overhead to income is higher, and so is the administrative overhead ratio. This may be a result of a planned set of expenses (e.g., a new computer system), or it may be due to decreased productivity that can drive up the relative impact of the expenses. Let's see if we can find out more.

Moving down the table to the Visit Info, we see that each year, the practice had an increase in the number of visits (or units of service) provided. We also see that the fees went up in FY3. However, in FY4, the amount collected per visit decreased by $10 compared with FY3 and is actually below what it was in FY2 before the fee increase. At the same time, there has been an increase in expenses per visit such that it is costing the practice more to provide each unit of service.

The confluence of decreased revenue and increased expenses per visit can be a recipe for disaster in the long run, as evidenced by data in the Net/Visit line. The figures show that the owner is actually making less per visit from FY1 to FY4.

What is happening in this practice is that over the past 4 years, it has expanded its clinical staff, collected less per visit, and had more expenses per visit. Additionally, there has not been a correspond-ing increase in production per full-time clinician. That figure has remained constant at 1,000 hours per year or 4.3 hours per day (1,000 hours / 46 weeks / 5 days).

From these data alone (that is, before we analyze the accounts receivable information), we can see that there are at least three major initiatives required to turn this around: (1) The amount collected per visit needs to increase, (2) the expenses per visit need to decrease, and (3) there needs to be more production per full-time clinician. If we had merely focused on what was billed and collected each year, we would have missed some important key indications that something was seriously problematic.

Let's now turn to Figure 3.3, Accounts Receivable. The total accounts receivable has grown considerably over the 4 years. This is likely also to be contributing to some of the problems we've noted. Moreover, when we examine the aged accounts receivable, we can see that in FY4,

47% of the total accounts receivable are more than 90 days old. This is compared with only 22% from FY1 and indicates that another business agenda item should be to address this in short order and make sure that the problems leading to the growing aged accounts receivable are addressed. Some practical initiatives that might be worth considering would be to examine whether copays are actively collected (an analysis by individual clinician may prove especially helpful as some clinicians might have more difficulty collecting payments from clients than others), resubmittals to insurance are done promptly, and attempts are made to make sure that individual account balances are not allowed to grow. A deeper analysis of each account would also be indicated here to see if the aged figures are due to just a few outlier accounts or are representative of a more pervasive difficulty with collections. In short, over the past 4 years, the amount collected per case has decreased by $733 per case.

Figure 3.3 Accounts Receivable

	FY1	FY2	FY3	FY4
Outstanding Dollars				
0-30 Days	$2,000	$2,250	$3,000	$4,500
31-60 Days	$1,500	$1,900	$2,750	$3,500
61-90 Days	$1,000	$1,500	$2,250	$2,000
91-120 Day	$500	$900	$1,500	$4,000
> 120 Days	$750	$1,200	$3,000	$5,000
Total	$5,750	$7,750	$12,500	$19,000
Percent of Total Outstanding				
0-30 Days	35%	29%	24%	24%
31-60 Days	26%	25%	22%	18%
61-90 Days	17%	19%	18%	11%
91-120 Day	9%	12%	12%	21%
> 120 Days	13%	15%	24%	26%
Total	100%	100%	100%	100%
CASE ORIGINATION				
Number of New Cases	30	55	80	100
New Cases/Clinician	30.00	36.67	40.00	40.00
Average Collected/Case	$3,733	$3,364	$3,250	$3,000

Clinician Comparisons

Although it is important to view the practice summary data within each year and across years, it is also important to zoom in and look at the productivity of individual clinicians. Many times, clues for the development of action plans can come from the patterns seen in the data of the individual clinical staff. Let's analyze the data for the different clinicians for this current year (Figure 3.4). First we examine their productivity information and then their accounts receivables.

Figure 3.4 Clinician Dashboard

STAFFING	Clinician 1	Clinician 2	Clinician 3	Self	Totals
Full-time equivalent	0.40	0.50	0.60	1.00	2.50
Days/Week on Site	2.00	2.50	3.00	5.00	
OVERALL INFO					
Total Billed	$60,000	$80,000	$110,000	$150,000	$400,000
Total Collected	$50,000	$50,000	$65,000	$135,000	$300,000
Collection Ratio	83%	63%	59%	90%	75%
Total Adjusted	$10,000	$30,000	$45,000	$15,000	$100,000
Adjustment Ratio	17%	38%	41%	10%	25%
Compensation %	0.50	0.52	0.55	0.00	
Compensation to Professional Staff	$25,000	$26,000	$35,750	0	$86,750
VISIT INFO					
Number of Billable Hours/Year	375	525	700	900	2500
Number of Billable Hours/Week (46 weeks)	8.2	11.4	15.2	19.6	54.3
Number of Billable Hours/Day (46 weeks)	4.1	4.6	5.1	3.9	4.3
$ Billed/Visit	$160	$152	$157	$167	$160
$ Collected/Visit	$133	$95	$93	$150	$120
$/Visit Compensation to Professional Staff	$66.67	$49.52	$51.07	$0	
$/Visit Income to Practice	$66.67	$45.71	$41.79	$150.00	
Other overhead expenses/visit	$45.60	$45.60	$45.60	$45.60	
Net to Practice/Visit	$21.07	$0.11	-$3.81	$104.40	
Net to Practice (Annual)	$7,900	$60	-$2,670		

As we begin to inspect these figures, we can see the following important differences among the four clinicians. The owner is the fourth clinician and labeled "Self." Examining the total billed, the clinicians who work more are billing more. This makes sense. However, on the next line, we can easily see that Clinician 1 and Clinician 2 collect the same amount, even though Clinician 2 works more hours. Clinician 1 also collects the largest percentage and adjusts out the least of what is billed compared with the other nonowners. There is a positive impact of this clinician having far fewer managed care patients as noted by the higher average collected per visit (far above most managed care contracted rates). At the same time, Clinician 1 is paid the least of the three clinicians both in terms of the percentage of collections and the actual dollars paid. For the sake of this demonstration, compensation is not allocated to the owner because the owner does not receive any guaranteed payments based on collections.

When we next look at the per visit information, we see that Clinician 1 is collecting more per visit and is bringing in far more compared with Clinicians 2 and 3 (the owner brings in the most because his or her compensation is excluded). In fact, in terms of its employees, the practice is annually making the most from Clinician 1 ($7,900) and almost at the break-even point for Clinician 2. The practice is actually losing money ($2,670) on Clinician 3. Without looking at these clinician-specific data, many owners would encourage all the clinicians to market and see more patients. However, it is doubtful that Clinicians 2 and 3 could actually produce meaningful profit to the practice even if they worked much harder (especially Clinician 3). Incentivizing these clinicians to do more of what they are doing, would not, after expenses (if their expenses increased proportionally), bring in much net revenue and would instead likely lead to more frustration in both the staff and owner. Rather, brainstorming needs to occur about how to have these clinicians engage in professional activities that are more profitable.

The data in Figure 3.4 indicate that it might make sense to help Clinicians 2 and 3 look to build additional streams of revenue that are compensated at a higher rate. They may or may not have to discontinue participation in managed care. Rather, they can increase other activities (e.g., developing a niche specialty, public speaking, running support groups, providing training seminars, etc.) that fall outside the purview of managed care (Walfish, 2010). This would enable them to earn more money by working harder *and* smarter.

What about Clinician 1? In looking at Figure 3.4, we would be very concerned about Clinician 1. We would wonder what the likelihood is that the person who has the worst compensation package, generates the most relative revenue, and pays the highest relative overhead of 50% (the percentage collected that goes to the practice is each clinician's overhead) would stay with the practice long term. To us, it makes sense to really focus on making sure this clinician feels adequately compensated and reinforced by the owner. Incentive programs or bonuses might be worth considering. Also, it might be advantageous to see whether Clinician 1 can increase the time allocated to the practice. There may even be some circumstances in which Clinician 1 can mentor Clinicians 2 and 3 and receive extra compensation based on the success and increased productivity of the other two clinicians.

Moving on to accounts receivable for each clinician (Figure 3.5), we can quickly spot another area that needs to be addressed.

Figure 3.5 Accounts Receivable by Clinician

	Clinician 1	Clinician 2	Clinician 3	Self	Totals
Outstanding Dollars					
0-30 Days	$100	$1,715	$2,400	$285	$4,500
31-60 Days	$100	$950	$2,100	$350	$3,500
61-90 Days	$50	$500	$1,250	$200	$2,000
91-120 Day	$500	$500	$2,600	$400	$4,000
> 120 Days	$75	$500	$4,225	$200	$5,000
Total	$825	$4,165	$12,575	$1,435	$19,000
Percent of Total Outstanding					
0-30 Days	12%	41%	19%	20%	24%
31-60 Days	12%	23%	17%	24%	18%
61-90 Days	6%	12%	10%	14%	11%
91-120 Day	61%	12%	21%	28%	21%
> 120 Days	9%	12%	34%	14%	26%
Total	100%	100%	100%	100%	100%
CASE ORIGINATION					
Number of New Cases	10	15	20	15	60
Average Collected/Case	$5,000	$3,333	$3,250	$9,000	$5,000

In both areas of this figure (the actual dollars and percentages), we can see that Clinician 3's collections that are more than 90 days old are out of line with the other clinicians' (including the owner). This accounts receivable difference may have to do with the clinician (not taking co-pays, allowing clients to build up balances due), particular clients (who are not paying deductible balances that are due), a problem with the billing office, or a problem with one of the contracted insurance plans. If this is not addressed, the almost $7,000 of monies that are outstanding for 90+ days will in all likelihood increase and not be collectible. Even if Clinician 3 is willing to tolerate a loss of 55% of the amount that would not normally be adjusted, the owner is losing the remaining 45% without having a corresponding decrease in overhead. By examining the individual clinician accounts receivables, it becomes immediately obvious where to look next to find what is contributing to the aged accounts.

We can also see the difference in the income that is being generated per case. From this vantage point, we can again see the impact of different practice patterns or payer mixes on the revenue produced.

In short, these three (current year, multiyear, and clinician) analyses are like a mosaic whose pieces, when put together, present a picture of the practice that provides the owner data for direction and avoids the illusion presented by only considering billed and collections figures.

four

Principles of Practice Management

In general, the time and effort you put into effectively running and managing your practice can produce a return for you both professionally and financially. This chapter focuses on the financial aspects of practice management.

The internal financial controls of your practice are the checks and balances you set up to protect your practice from inefficiencies, unnecessary loss of revenue, missed opportunities, and potential threats. From a financial point of view, you need to know what is going on in your practice: Who is responsible for billing, collecting, and paying the bills? Does one person have all the control over these functions? If so, how do you assure yourself that all of these functions are being handled without theft? Theft happens, sometimes by the people you come to entrust the most. In a larger office, you can have division of duties such that the person collecting payments at the front window is not the person recording those payments in your practice management system. This division of duties allows you more peace of mind that all of your cash collections are being properly recorded, especially if the clinician is recording the receipt of the co-payment that is handled by the receptionist. Even with the division of duties, you need to create a monthly reconciliation that you can review to make sure all of the cash payments to the practice have been properly deposited and recorded.

However, in many smaller offices, this division of job responsibilities is not always possible. So how do you protect yourself and your business? In this situation, *you* become the checks and balances person, using systematic procedures. Here are some general systems that every small practice should have.

Weekly Oversight Meetings

Set up weekly, monthly, and quarterly meetings to review reports with your office manager. The weekly meetings generally need only be about 15 minutes long. Once a month, there should be an extended meeting to review monthly financial reports with the office manager.

Weekly meetings should include, at a minimum, review of the following reports generated by your office manager or billing service.

Weekly Vendor Report: Which vendors were paid over the last week, what were the bills for, and what was the due date of each bill (are you paying early, late, or on time)? New vendors should be highlighted each week along with documentation such as address, purpose of vendor, and how this vendor was chosen. Why is this information important? You should always look carefully into the backgrounds and reputations of new vendors to make sure they function professionally and independently of your staff (and are not your office manager's relative or friend). If you are paying vendors too early, this could have an impact on your cash flow in the next week or two. Paying vendors late indicates cash flow problems or an inefficient staff that is not paying attention to detail. This may also be accompanied by a late fee payment. Either way, it's troubling. The weekly vendor report should be printed directly from your financial accounting software. A report that is not from the software could have been modified without your knowing. Be clear with your office manager about when you want each bill to be paid.

Cash Balance Report: This shows your current cash balance in your checking and savings accounts. It needs to be compared with your actual bank balances to make sure there is not a major variance. Of course, the bank might have a different amount due to deposited checks that have not cleared, as well as checks you have written that have not yet been deposited by the payee.

Unpaid Vendor Report: This report shows the bills that are currently in the system but not paid and when are they due. This, along with your cash balance, will help you determine your ability to pay your bills over the next month.

Next Payroll Date and Anticipated Cash Needs for Payroll Report: This report shows the gross amount you need to pay, including compensation and employer tax payments. It is essential that you know the exact amount you need to have in the account from which payroll funds are drawn. There are often strict statutes governing the necessity of paying your employees on time.

Reconciliation of Cash/Checks Received to the Practice Management System Report: This report should show you the proof that what was collected and deposited into the bank matches what is in your practice management system. Generally, we recommend that you personally collect the receipts each day and make the deposit yourself. That way you know exactly what was deposited and can double-check the weekly production logs and the practice management system to make sure the totals match.

Monthly Oversight Meetings

In the monthly meeting you would ask for the current week's reports as well as the following.

Bank Reconciliation Report: This report is generated by your financial accounting software. It will tell you if there are outstanding checks that have not cleared (as well as checks that were not deposited due to insufficient funds) and provide you with the opportunity to review this with the office manager. Look at outstanding deposits. In general, a deposit that is outstanding more than a few days is a trigger for concern. Was a deposit recorded twice? Did a deposit not actually get to the bank? This needs immediate attention because you do not have the cash balance you thought you did. If you are paying bills believing you have cash that you don't, you will be bouncing checks all over town.

Reconciliation Report of Cash/Checks Received to the Practice Management System: This is the monthly reconciliation of the funds collected and entered into the practice management system. You need to make sure these match with the records you have of what you deposited weekly. For example, if the practice received $1,000 cash over the course of the month, you want to make sure you can see this in the practice management system as well as in your bank reconciliation.

Monthly Vendor Report: This is similar to the weekly report. In fact, you should compare this monthly report to your weekly reports to make sure the vendors are the same. Although one never wants to be suspicious of your administrative staff, if you only get a weekly report, it would be easy for someone to print a vendor check with a previous date on it after the weekly vendor report was run. In doing this, the staff member would be bypassing your checks and balances system.

Review the Monthly Practice Management Report: What are the aged accounts receivables? Are you collecting in a timely fashion from self-pay patients? Are your clinicians/office staff members collecting co-pays where appropriate? Is a particular insurance company not paying in a timely manner? Are the clinician's billings appropriate for their schedules and the amount of time you are allocating office space to each one? There may not be clear answers to these questions, but this will facilitate discussion and points for your office manager to research.

Quarterly Oversight Meetings

On a quarterly basis you should add the following reports to your meetings.

Balance Sheet: Your balance sheet shows the assets and liabilities of your practice. As you review the balance sheet, look specifically at the cash and debts of the practice. If you had to take out a loan to start the business, you want to keep an eye on the balance. Along with making the regular payments on the loan, is there a plan to pay back the loan early? How might that be accomplished? If you have multiple debts, which debts would be important to pay back first? Sometimes when we are busy with the professional aspects of the practice, we forget to look at its net worth, which comprises both assets and debts. This report will keep you in the habit of reviewing you financial position each quarter. Please see Chapter 2 for a more detailed explanation of this report.

Profit and Loss Statement—Budget Versus Actual: As you compare these two columns on the report, you should look for significant variances. Do you know why you are above or below budget? This is important because as it can tell you what to keep doing and what you may need to change. Are there management and strategic planning decisions that need to be made due to these variances? Are the variances due to timing of payments (e.g., a large annual payment that you made this month that skews the report for the month but will average out over the course of the year), vacation schedules of clinicians, ineffective billing procedures? Are there possibly more significant factors that need research before you can get to a decision point?

Clinician's Receipts Versus Budgeted Receipts: Here, you can see whether your clinicians are meeting or beating the productivity goals that have been set. This creates a discussion point with them as well as some insight into budget issues.

New Patient Report: This is another important report because it looks at the flow of patients as they come into the practice. It shows you the new patients and to whom have they been referred and assigned. You need this information to determine whether referrals are going only to specific clinicians and, if so, why. If your system can also show you whether the patient was referred to the practice in general or a specific clinician, and the basic demographics of the patients, referral partners, and third-party payers you can obtain important information about what types of patients are going to which clinicians. As discussed in Chapter 3, this can help you ensure that there is a balance and flow of cases that seem appropriate based on the skills and specialties of your clinical staff.

Additional Strategies for Internal Controls

Reconcile the Daily (Weekly) Receipts: Many offices use a log sheet listing the patients seen and the charge, amount of co-pay required to be collected and what is collected. The form of payment (cash, check, and charge) should also be included. If a co-pay is not collected at the time of visit, a reason should be listed on the sheet. There should be a required co-pay policy in your office. However, occasionally there are lapses: Patients leave their wallets at home; your receptionist or clinician may forget to ask for payment; a patient may storm out of the office without paying. However, these types of lapses should be the exception, not the rule. You should review this process and the log sheets occasionally. Rather than reviewing log sheets at your monthly meeting, ask for a copy of the reconciliation and the log sheet on a random day once a month, so that your staff knows to keep it correctly updated at all times.

Be Observant: Sometimes we get so wrapped up in providing professional services that we have blinders on as to what is happening in the rest of the office. We may be marketing and providing services, but not fully aware of what is happening in the business. Sometimes listening (or overhearing) is critical to knowing what is going on in your office. Was your office manager's spouse recently laid off, leading to real personal cash flow pressures? Does a staff person have a sick parent or child that distracts them from the boring task of posting transactions when he or she is in the office? In addition to listening, you should always be looking around the office as you go from point A to point B. Occasionally sit at an office manager's or billing person's desk. Take a quick view of work that is sitting around uncompleted. Are there insurance denials sitting in a desk drawer that have not been attended? Are there multiple unreturned phone call messages sitting on the desk? These "finds" are important to the front-desk operations and collections for the practice.

All of these situations could create problems that negatively affect your bottom line. If payroll cannot be met, you will not take a paycheck and maybe even have to put money into the practice. That's right—you. The impact of not paying attention to *how* the practice is running is the sting of having to personally make a financial contribution into the practice (or work for reduced compensation or for free).

Other Strategies

Maximizing Income: This should always be at the forefront of your practice management thoughts. How can the practice maximize its income without increasing your fixed costs? Some questions to consider:

- What are your current service lines? These can be categorized by clinician, type of service, or even different types of specialized treatment programs. Can you determine what areas create a net income for the practice? This may not be the program or service that has either the highest reimbursement (if its costs are higher) or conversely the one that has the lower reimbursement (if its costs are correspondingly less). It is crucial to look at the net or bottom line (i.e., income – expenses).

- Are there needs in the community that are not being met? How might you tap into those community needs?

- How might another location suit your needs, and to what extent will the increased income be offset by the cost of the new location?

- What are the practice's referral patterns—both referrals into your practice and those that flow out of the practice to other professionals? Are there services that you are typically referring patients to that you could gear up and provide? Are there referrals partners that are not currently active and should be? Do you need to build new relationships or reinvigorate old ones?

- How are the productivity goals set for the clinicians? Are productivity goals even set for the clinician? Do you postpone these meetings because they are uncomfortable? Do you view them as an awful chore? Or do you view them as a step to making sure you enhance the accuracy of the budgeting process? What are the incentives for your professional staff to reach their goals? How do they grow their practices within your practice? How do you help them grow their practice?

- How are the productivity goals set for your administrative staff? Your administrative staff members have an impact on the bottom line as well. Are they collecting fees at the time of the visit? Are they getting billing done frequently and promptly? Are they pursuing accounts so they don't age? Are they demonstrating world-class "customer service" to your clients and referral partners, or do they just think so? Most people believe they are delivering excellent customer service, but the data suggest that only a small percentage of people actually do so (Crosby & Johnson, 2006).

Reducing Expenses: Running a practice is hard work and takes much time. You are not always able to study every line item in your budget in detail to reduce its costs. However, when preparing your budget, you can look to two to three line items that you feel have increased more than expected over the years. Take these items and plan to have you or your office manager determine, with research, whether there is a way to reduce these costs. Examples of areas that you can find reductions typically are the following:

- Telephone: Get quotes and try to negotiate with your current carrier.
- Office supplies: Price shop the top 10 items you purchase to make sure you are getting the best prices. Are you purchasing in volume (which generally means lower cost) or only purchasing when a particular supply is running low?
- Insurance: Get price quotes of your general business insurances (e.g., premises, health, life, disability, workers compensation, and even malpractice) at least every couple of years. Make sure you are comparing similar coverages with your current policies.
- Billing or collection services: You can price shop here as well. Be sure to have written agreements with these agencies that clearly spell out their charges and add-ons and how and in what form you get your data if you terminate the relationship. You also can meet with your agency occasionally and ask for better pricing.

Clinician Employment Contracts: The days of hiring someone by handshake have long passed. You and your employees and independent contractors (if applicable) have an agreement—a contract of sorts. They will work for you as long as they want and you will compensate them with an agreed-on wage and benefits. However, the specifics need to be clear. What are the benefits you pay and at what percentage of the total cost? What are the conditions of the wage? Is it by the hour, by number of patients seen, by a percentage of what is collected? What do you expect of your employees? What are the violations that may lead to termination? What is the process for dealing with a problem? Your expectations of one another should be spelled out in detail. What happens when an employee leaves the practice? How do you part ways in an ethical manner in terms of patient care and also from a financial standpoint? Part of being clear (with both clinical and administrative staff) is to set expectations at the start of the employer–employee relationship and, we hope, to avoid the costs of litigation at the end of that relationship. Such costs are often not in your budget and can easily amount to tens of thousands dollars. Hiring an attorney in this area of your practice can help you be more confident that your employment contracts are clear, address your interests, and are enforceable.

Managing Cash Flow: Cash flow can be difficult to manage if the practice is not adequately funded from the outset. Most practices are not well capitalized because they start as a one- or two-person operation that invests more time than cash (often called "sweat equity") in the business. If this is the case for you, it becomes even more critical to watch the cash flow and plan for large expenses or expenses that may only occur once a year. When looking at available cash, you also need to look out 3 to 6 months to see what additional bills may be coming. These expenses need to budgeted or planned for so you do not end up short of cash when the expense becomes payable. For example, if you know you have an annual charge of $6,000 due in March each year, you will need to plan to have that cash available to make that payment on time. Otherwise you might end up needing to dip into your line of credit (and pay interest charges) or pay all or part of the $6,000 from your personal funds. Cash flow planning and budgeting go hand in hand. This is much easier to do when you have a workable budget to refer to when making cash decisions.

Managing Debt: You need to understand how debt or general obligations affect your cash flow. When deciding to seek a loan for your practice, the first step is to determine that you have the ability to repay the loan, which you can estimate by reviewing your cash flow and budget. If it's not clear how the practice will repay the loan, then you should reconsider applying for a loan.

When analyzing loan options consider the following factors:

Annual Percentage Rate (APR)—This is the full cost of the loan, including loan fees expressed in terms of yearly percentage rate. All lenders must compute this percentage the same way, so it is a good tool in comparing loan options.

Amortization—Loan amortization is the calculation of the equal periodic payment necessary to pay off over the term of the loan. There is a listing you can request from the lender that shows how much of each payment goes to pay the interest on the loan and how much is applied toward the principal. It should also show the total paid in interest. This can help you evaluate the impact of different options based on the amount, duration, and interest rate of the loan.

Fixed Versus Variable Interest—Will your interest rate be fixed throughout the term of the loan? Or will the rate change? If so, how often and by how much?

Closing Costs—These are costs incurred to get the loan, such as appraisals, application fees, loan fees, for example. You will need to decide how you will pay these fees. Do you have the cash to pay them outright, or will you be rolling them into the loan and thus increasing your monthly payments? Whenever possible, it makes sense to pay these fees at the closing and not roll them into the total loan proceeds.

When deciding on taking a loan to purchase assets, you will need to discuss any tax implications with your accountant. How you use the loan money may have an impact on your taxable income for the year of the initial loan and the years when the loan is being repaid.

Loans and leases take many different forms, such as:

- Equipment loans: These are typically term loans with a fixed interest rate and term. Loans are often secured by the equipment you are purchasing. Equipment loans are typically for purchasing expensive or large amounts of equipment or software.

- Line of credit loans: These are loans to help with cash flow in a practice. It is always prudent to have a line of credit loan for your business to protect against a cash crunch. This might happen if your largest insurance provider held back payments for 4 weeks or you had a data system failure where your bills were not submitted for 2 weeks before you noticed it or had the problem corrected. A line of credit would allow you to draw from the loan to meet your financial obligations in the business while you correct the problem. An important point to keep in mind regarding a line of credit is that it should not be used to fund larger purchases. Most credit lines require that you have a period of 30 days each year when the balance is zero for the bank to see that this is not a term loan disguised as a line of credit. This would mean you would have to repay the loan in full sometime within 12 months.

- Building or leasehold improvement loans: These are loans to fund a purchase of a building or the tenant improvements when you move into a new office. Such a loan can be initiated during the startup phase of a practice or after a practice is established and wishes to move to different space. The term of these loans may range from 10 to 20 years depending on the amount borrowed and the finances of the deal. Building or leasehold improvement loans most likely have a fixed interest rate but may also be variable. Some banks are currently resetting these rates every 3 years. This building or office improvement loan tends to be a loan project with substantial costs, and your repayment ability needs to be proven to the bank to receive the loan.

- Operating leases: These are disguised rental agreements for a predetermined period of time. You pay a monthly fee for the use of the piece of equipment (a copier, for example). At the end of the lease term, the company picks up the equipment, and you either lease or buy another copier from the same leasing company or another vendor or purchase your current copier for fair market value from the lease company. You are obligated for the entire lease term even if you return the equipment early. You should also be fully aware of your lease terms regarding maintenance and upkeep to avoid large fees at the end of the lease term for repairs. Always document the lease terms initially and review them annually to make sure you are complying with the terms of the agreement.

- Capital equipment leases: These leases are in essence financing agreements. You make payments over the term of the lease and buy the equipment for $1 at the end of the term. In effect, you have purchased the equipment through your payments over the lease term.

- Office rental leases: Office leases can take different forms. Some leases are inclusive of all expenses, including utilities. This type of lease is not common and typically works best when you are renting space in an established office. Some leases require you to pay the base rent and the operating expenses that relate directly to your space, such as utilities and basic maintenance. Other leases (triple net leases) require you to pay the stated rent and all of the expenses of the property including utilities, real estate taxes, and insurance. It may be helpful to ask for examples of what this triple net cost has been over the past 3 to 5 years, as we have known some practices to have "sticker shock" when presented with a large bill long after they have signed the initial lease. When comparing lease costs or renegotiating a lease, you need to understand which type of lease you have and what expenses, as the tenant, you will be responsible to pay. Some leases charge an annual fee called a *common area maintenance* (CAM) charge. This allows the landlord to pass the general maintenance of the common areas of the building to the tenants based on the percentage of total space rented by each tenant. When negotiating the lease, you may want to state a maximum CAM charge allowed per year to be sure that you do not have significant surprises when the year-end CAM charge bill comes your way.

If you are considering an outright purchase versus a capital (or financing) lease or loan, carefully consider all your options. You can calculate the interest rate in the capital lease by knowing the cost of the equipment if you were to buy it outright. For example, let's assume the cost to purchase the equipment outright is $10,000 and the lease option they are giving you is $198 per month for 5 years, with a $1 purchase option at the end of the lease term. By using a loan calculator, you can determine that the lease option has a 7% interest rate built into the contract. Over the period of the lease, you would have paid approximately $1,880 in interest in addition to the $10,000 purchase price. You can compare this to the financing rates you can obtain in the open market with your current bank to determine which might be a better financing option.

Before signing any loan or leasing agreement, be sure to fully understand the terms and conditions (i.e., what can sometimes be confusing and in fine print). These documents/agreements obligate the company (and possibly you and your family, if you signed personally). Read the terms of your loan. These are called *loan covenants* for a reason. Be absolutely sure you understand your obligations and the lender's freedoms (e.g., ability to demand payment in full). If you are not sure, be sure to speak with your accountant and attorney to get input.

Do not presume that the bank officer has given you all the necessary information for you to understand the fine points around the loan. They represent the lender and, even if well intentioned, may not be fully informed. For example, in some cases, banks require that you meet certain criteria to keep the loan in good standing and not force a default. They may want quarterly or yearly financial statements (both business and personal). They may want listings of your accounts receivable (remember to delete patient names from these reports to protect client confidentiality). They may require that you not take out other debt (including credit cards) without getting their permission first. Read the terms and make sure you adhere to them. The worst-case scenario is to have them demand immediate repayment in full for not reaching or meeting the covenants or terms within the loan.

Banks consider many factors when determining whether to issue a loan to a given applicant. Here are a few such factors:

- **Collateral:** Banks want to know there is some backing to the loan should it go into default. What assets does the practice have for collateral? Equipment and accounts receivable tend to be the items they look to in a medical practice. However, mental health practices often do not have much equity in the furnishings and other equipment (for example, compared with a dental practice). Although banks will look at your accounts receivable when evaluating whether to issue the loan, they typically prefer to rely on equipment and other hard assets for the collateral. In general, banks do not like to use accounts receivable as collateral for a loan because the collateral is not an easy asset for them to retrieve should a company default on a note (as you have probably experienced yourself when trying to collect on older accounts receivables). Most mental health practices do not have enough collateral for their loan requests. Thus, the bank will usually ask for personal financial statements and a personal guarantee. In many cases they may want to use your home or other owned real estate as collateral. This means that if the business defaults on the loan, your personal assets may be attached (i.e., become the legal property of the bank).

- **Credit History:** Banks will look at your prior credit history as part of their due diligence in determining whether to approve your loan application. They will look at your history with their bank and will look at prior lending patterns as well.

- **Ability to Repay the Loan:** Does the practice generate the cash flow necessary to repay the loan? What is the business plan regarding the reason for the loan? How will the equipment being purchased increase your cash flow? These are all questions you should be ready to answer when applying for a loan. In addition, many banks will ask for your historical financial statements (i.e., often 2 to 3 years of tax returns, balance sheets, and profit and loss statement) and a projected financial statement (sometimes call a *pro forma*) that will show the bank your ability to repay the loan in the future. Always be ready with a professional-looking written business plan that addresses your need for the loan, the intended purpose of the loan, and what funds will be available to repay it.

How It All Fits Together

The key to efficient practice management is staying involved and asking questions. Make sure you understand the roles and abilities of the staff you trust with practice management details. Be mindful and put in the energy to oversee the business and meet with your office manager. Never stop asking questions. Your attention to detail will model for others that you expect the same attention to detail from them.

five

Compensation

This chapter mainly focuses on compensation for employees who are not owners. We also briefly discuss owner compensation models. But first let's start with some basics on compensation models and the definition of compensation.

Compensation is the total of what a person receives for the work he or she performs. It includes wages, fringe benefits, bonuses, and paid time off. Many employees view their compensation as only the money they bring home on a weekly or biweekly basis. They don't see themselves as receiving a compensation package. It is important to make sure your employees understand the dollar cost to the practice of other benefits that the practice provides to them. Some practices, on a yearly basis, present their employees with a statement of compensation. This statement would include the base salary, cost to the employer of health insurance premiums, pension contributions, disability or life insurance premiums, bonuses, and paid time off. As a professional office, you may also provide employees with other benefits such as professional development costs, licensing fees, and malpractice insurance. If you provide these benefits, they should also be included in the employee's statement of compensation.

Employee Compensation

From the federal Department of Labor and the Internal Revenue Service (IRS) point of view, most staff working for you will be labeled as *employees* (not *independent contractors*). The IRS has a 20-factor test to determine whether someone is an employee or an independent contractor. The IRS looks to your control over the staff members in your office as to what work they perform, when they do it, and how they do it. The end result of this test is that most, if not all, the staff members in your practice will be deemed to be employees, even if they are part time or have other jobs. In most cases, you will be handling the billing, patient referrals, and scheduling for all of your clinicians, and this is enough to give you the control the IRS looks for in making the employee versus independent contractor determination. The IRS and the federal and state labor departments audit employers, including mental health practices. A failed audit can result in the practice being responsible for payroll taxes not properly withheld, the employer's portion of payroll taxes, plus penalties and interest. This can easily run into the tens of thousands of dollars if you have many employees (e.g., own a group practice).

How you pay your administrative staff is fairly easy because most of these employees will probably be paid on an hourly base rate (they are called *nonexempt* employees). Your office manager could be on an annual salary (this would called an *exempt* employee) because this person supervises the rest of your staff and is exempt from being paid overtime wages. For office staff to be on a salary base or exempt, rather than hourly compensation model, you would need to show that they have supervisory responsibilities. An hourly employee would need to be paid overtime at a higher rate for all hours worked over 40 hours in any week. Salaried employees typically do not get paid overtime. However, they may be eligible for a bonus or incentive plan. As a caveat to this discussion, both federal and state labor laws are always changing, often to benefit the employees. Any changes to your payroll methodology should be reviewed by a professional who is familiar with current labor laws in your state.

Some practices offer bonuses or incentive compensation for administrative staff members to reward them for contributing to significant and positive changes to the business—for example, creating goals on collections of co-pays or better managing the accounts receivable. All administrative staff should receive an evaluation at the same time each year. Take time to provide constructive feedback and praise. Like most people, your administrative staff likes to feel appreciated. Discussions regarding raises should be tied to their performance appraisal.

Compensation for your clinical staff is a little more complex. Do you pay them a straight salary, an hourly rate, or a percentage of their collections? Each practice may have a different compensation model. These models are the policy or blueprint each practice follows for providing compensation to their clinical staff. In most mental health practices, clinicians are paid a percentage of their collections. The collection percentage varies from practice to practice but is typically in the range of 40% to 60%.

How do you decide on the compensation in your practice? First, review your overhead expenses, as noted in Chapter 2. The percentage of collections that is kept by the practice needs to cover both direct (malpractice insurance, fringe benefits, etc.) and indirect (rent, office expenses, utilities, etc.) expenses. In addition, you should maintain a cushion to cover unanticipated expenses as well as additional profit to the owner(s). Given that supporting and administering a practice requires much time and expertise, the owner should be compensated for the extra duties and oversight. If you don't derive revenue from the clinicians who work for you, you may eventually resent their presence, which in turn could have an impact on office morale and general trust.

After deciding how much you need to earn from your clinical staff to cover overhead and extra compensation for yourself, the next step is to find out what other mental practices are paying clinicians. You need to be competitive to attract the most competent and highly motivated clinicians. Remember, these professionals will represent you to your referral partners.

In determining a compensation package, a higher percentage of fees collected does not necessarily translate into higher net pay for your professional employee. For example, let's say Practice A sees mainly patients who are covered by managed care. Their average collection per clinical hour is $90. If the practice pays its clinician 60%, that clinician would make $54 per clinical hour. On the other hand, Practice B collects an average of $150 per hour and pays its clinician 50%. That clinician would make $75 per clinical hour. If all the other benefits were exactly the same for both practices, and both employees billed 30 hours per week for 46 weeks a year, the clinician in Practice B would make $28,980 more per year than the clinician in Practice A, even though the compensation percentage is lower in Practice B. Furthermore, Practice A would have $49,680 of gross income from its employee (40% of $90 × 30 hours/week × 46 weeks). Practice B would have $103,500 of gross income from its employee (50% of $150 × 30 hours/week × 46 weeks).

In addition, you need to make sure from an overhead perspective that you know what the direct costs will be and what the incremental costs are for adding an additional clinician. Examples of incremental costs would be additional malpractice premiums, the cost of hiring another administrative person, any electronic health record (EHR) costs that are on a per provider basis, coffee and snacks consumed by the clinicians and their clients, increased utility costs if they work at alternative times when most clinicians are not in the office (e.g., evenings, weekends).

Once you have determined the incremental costs, you will know what would be left for a contribution to the general overhead based on your income projections for the clinician.

For example, let's say you expect a new clinician who has a following to produce $160,000 in collections over her first year. If you were to pay her 48% of collections, there would be 52% of the collections or $83,200 left in the practice for expenses. Now assume the following hypothetical incremental costs:

- Health insurance—employer contribution = $3,500
- Payroll taxes and other fringe benefits—10% of compensation = $7,680
- Malpractice insurance increase—$500
- EHR costs per clinician—$960
- Additional part-time staffing costs—$5,600

After the incremental costs there would be profit before overhead of $64,960. This will allow you to evaluate this number along with the total general overhead to determine whether this clinician would cover her representative share of the general overhead.

There are two other methods of paying professionals employed by your practice that are less common. The first is paying a straight salary. For this compensation model to be profitable to the practice, you would need a steady source of patients that can be scheduled with the employed clinician. Some practices provide a salary to a new clinician just out of school to give them an opportunity to build their clinical practice but still bring home enough compensation to live on. The practice needs to know that they are underwriting the ramp-up period while that clinician is working far under capacity. In such cases the employment contract should specify a time when the clinician would then move to a production-based system.

The second alternative method for compensating professionals is a per-session fee. In this method, the clinician is paid for every clinical hour provided (regardless of what is collected). Although similar to the collections percentage basis in that the clinician is being paid for billable time, it does not take into account the types of reimbursement sources for patients the clinician is seeing. Are these patients all covered by insurance where the collections to the practice are less than full fee? You would need to develop an accurate projection of the mix of payers to determine the proper per-session fee. You would also need to continue to monitor any changes in the clinician's practice to be sure you are not losing money on this compensation structure. This system is hard to manage, which is why we rarely see this method of compensation.

Owner's Compensation

There are various compensation models for a practice with multiple owners. In some practices, owner compensation is allocated on the basis of ownership percent. Others are based on some model of productivity. Your model should be tailored to your practice's unique needs (which may change over time). Let's look at some general models.

Compensation Based on Ownership

We see this model less in business today than we did many years ago. When practices were started with multiple partners who were all equal investors and shareholders, this model could make sense. In many ways, it was an "all for one, and one for all" approach. The model divides the net income of the practice, before owner's compensation, and allocates this amount to the owners on the basis of their percentage of ownership. This model does not take into consideration productivity of owners or management duties of owners. If you own 60% of the company, you will earn 60% of the profits. In cases where productivity is different, this model often leads to dissatisfaction among some of the owners.

Production-Based Compensation Models

In some productivity models, the practice allocates the net available income for owner compensation based on an agreed-on productivity model. The model is usually based on either practice billings or practice collections. The difference between the two can be substantial. When you calculate firm billings, you are basically focusing on clinical hours worked, assuming all of the charges for work are consistent across the practice. If you assume that every clinician bills at $150 per 1-hour visit, then the billings method of allocation will define the time allocated to the practice solely in clinical hours. Even though two owners work the same number of clinical hours, their collections to the practice could be very different—for example, if one owner is on insurance panels and accepts $90 per hour for service (discounted from the regular fee of $150) and another owner has no insurance patients and sees all self-pay patients at $150 for that same hour of work.

The key question is what is right for your practice? Some practices have a values structure that says the partners should all be treated equally based on time and energy devoted to (not dollars generated for) the practice. This would lend itself to a billings percent allocation. Some practices want to reward those partners who generate more revenue for the practice. This situation would lend itself to a collections allocation.

Hybrid Methods

Many practices use a hybrid method for allocating the income generated. In some cases, the practice first allocates a portion of each owner's profits based on their percentage of ownership and then adds to it an amount based on production. For example, 20% of the profit could be allocated by ownership percent and 80% based on the collections of the owners. In essence, there would be two "buckets of funds." If in this example, there were $300,000 available to the partners, $60,000 would be dispersed according to ownership percent. The remaining $240,000 would be dispersed as a ratio of productivity based on what the partners collected or billed depending on the model adopted by the entity.

However, this would not recognize partners' work that does not directly bring income into the practice (e.g., supervising clinical and administrative staff, conducting clinical research, hiring, negotiating business relationships, working on the practice website, building referral relationships). Such work allows the other owners to spend more time with patients. Therefore, some practices also provide a guaranteed amount to each owner who spends time managing the practice.

In some cases, the allocation becomes fine-tuned by allocating income received by each partner to them directly and then deducting every expense paid either directly, if it is a direct cost, or allocating general expenses among many partners based on an agreed percentage amount. This methodology (called *cost accounting*) allows everyone to see what their bottom line income is, which is the amount that would be available to draw in compensation. This method can be extremely cumbersome (and more expensive) from an accounting perspective because every expense needs to be reviewed for the appropriate allocation to the owners and overhead. It is rare that a mental health practice chooses this accounting method.

How It All Fits Together

The method used to determine owner compensation should be clearly defined and written in the legal agreements for each professional and perhaps in the bylaws, operating agreement, and policies and procedures documents of the practice. Many partner conflicts revolve around the differing concepts of "fair" compensation. It is imperative that there is a clear methodology from the beginning and a mechanism in the operating agreement for review of the compensation model and when and under what circumstances it can be changed.

Each practice needs to find its right compensation model. These models should consider what skills each owner brings to the practice and how productive each owner is, however productivity is defined (e.g., direct collections received; indirect support of the practice). A model that incorporates productivity, is aligned with the culture of the practice, and respects the skills that each owner brings to the endeavor will be the starting point of a long-term profitable and productive practice.

six

Saving for Retirement

As a long-term personal goal, you should be saving money for your retirement throughout your "earning" years. Although there are times when this may not be possible, the old adage of "pay yourself first" rings true here. It is important to make this a priority throughout your professional career because you cannot plan to rely solely on Social Security as your only income source in retirement. Ideally you would save enough for your retirement years without counting on other sources of income such as Social Security. Taking charge of your long-range financial security will allow you to sleep at night knowing that you have put in place a plan to enjoy your retirement years without worrying about money.

There are a number of programs that allow for pretax contributions to a long-term retirement plan. These are often called *pension plans* but may also be called a *retirement plans* or a *profit-sharing plans*. Many times, the terms are used interchangeably.

As a single practitioner or a group practitioner, there are many options for funding your retirement. Your level of ability to fund a retirement plan will determine the type of plan that you adopt. You need to complete some due diligence in determining the right retirement (pension) plan for your business. Here are some basic questions to ask and information you need to gather to make the right decision:

1. First evaluate your own retirement needs.
2. Create an employee census (a list of employee with their ages and time in service).

3. Determine the goals of the retirement plan for both the owner and the employees.
4. Determine how much, if any, the company would contribute to the plan for employees.
5. Speak with a pension consultant or accountant to get some options of plans available to meet the needs and criteria listed in items 1 through 4.

Once you have the information needed, you can choose from a menu of plans that meets the current needs. Remember, you can always adjust the plan as your needs or the employees' needs change over the years.

Here we focus on plans related to two employer situations. First, we discuss retirement plans for solo practices that do not have employees (i.e., for just the business owner or owners). Second, we discuss retirement plans for practices with up to 50 employees. Remember, the details we provide (percentages, limits, etc.) are as of the writing of this book. Be sure to check on current laws relating to pension plan contribution limits.

Retirement Plans With No Employees

There are three common types of plans for owner only retirement plans.

1. **Simplified Employee Pension (SEP):** This plan allows the owner to contribute to the plan up to 25% of his or her net income each year up to a maximum of $53,000. Because the deduction to the plan is used in this 25% computation, the actual contribution will be 20% after computing the algebraic formula. This plan is simple to administer because there are no annual filings. The plan is typically set up with prototype documents from investment firms. There is no requirement to fund the pension each year, and you can fund at any level up to the 25% of net income. You are not required to contribute the maximum each year. The benefits to this type of plan are the flexibility of the funding options each year and that there are no separate tax filings. The downside is that your contributions

are limited to a percent of your net income, which may limit the amount you were hoping to put into the plan.

2. **Owner-Only 401(k):** This plan allows you to contribute 25% of the net income (because the deduction to the plan is used in this 25% computation, the actual contribution will be 20% after computing the algebraic formula) plus $18,000 salary deferral, plus $6,000 catch-up contribution if over age 50. In this plan, the maximum contribution is $53,000 or $59,000 if you are over age 50. Although similar to the SEP, the benefit of this plan is that it allows for a larger deferral of income into your plan when your income is below the $265,000 level. This plan also does not require any contributions each year. There may be some administrative costs to set up this type of plan and ongoing yearly fees to maintain the plan documents.

3. **Defined Benefit Plan:** This plan funds the pension according to an assumed monthly benefit at retirement age; for example, funding the plan to create a $1,000 monthly benefit to the owner at age 65 for the rest of his or her life. This type of plan is used when a business owner consistently has earnings in excess of $100,000 and has a high commitment to funding the retirement plan. The plan has minimum funding requirements each year and once the plan is established, the plan needs to stay in place for at least 3 years. A defined benefit plan comes with a higher cost of administration, as an actuary needs to run the calculations each year to determine the amount of funding to reach the monthly benefit goal. This type of plan is used most often in the last few years before retirement when a practitioner has significant earnings and needs less cash at present to live. This plan would allow for some significant contributions in the last few years before retirement.

Retirement Plans for Practices With Employees

If you have employees working for you, there are various options to consider.

1. **1. SEP:** This plan follows the same rules as explained in the owner-only section. However, the downside when you have employees is that you need to contribute the same percent of compensation for each of the employees as you contribute for yourself as the owner. This can become costly to the employer and would likely be a disadvantage if you were trying to curtail some of your out-of-pocket costs for employee benefits. Administration of the plan is simple because there are no annual filings or complex pension calculations to be completed. The plan is typically set up with prototype documents from investment firms. There is no requirement to fund each year, and you can fund at any level up to the 25%. Because the deduction to the plan is used in this 25% computation, the actual contribution will be 20% after computing the algebraic formula. You are not required to contribute the maximum each year. All participants also have their own accounts where they can manage the investment of the contributions provided by the company. The employees are also immediately vested in any contributions you make. This means the full amount of the contribution is available to them should they leave the practice. Most employers set up this plan requiring that an employee work for the practice for 3 years before being eligible for company contributions into the plan. In general, practices want to avoid funding for temporary or short-term employees as they are (in this type of plan) vested immediately in the funds you contribute for them.

2. **Simple IRA Plan:** This plan allows your employees to contribute $12,500 ($15,500 if over age 50) of their compensation each year into the plan on a tax-deferred basis. The employer is required either to match dollar for dollar up to 3% of compensation or contribute 2% of all eligible employees' compensation to the plan. This plan allows you to require up to a 2-year service requirement to be eligible for the plan. You can also require that employees have a salary of at least $5,000 per year before they become eligible to be a participant in the plan.

This can eliminate some part-time employees. A Simple IRA plan is easy to set up, typically with a prototype plan from an investment company. There is no annual filing requirement to the government, so the administrative costs are low.

In addition to the SEP and Simple plans, there are plans specifically designed to meet the company's needs and goals. These plans fall into two broad categories: defined contribution plans and defined benefit plans.

3. **Defined Contribution Plans:** These plans are common in the small business world. They allow the company to design the plan to meet its current needs and goals. For example, a company may want to have a retirement plan that is more beneficial to the older employees in the business. In many cases, the contributions can be changed year to year and are not mandatory. Many of these plans are set to maximize the owner's contribution and minimize the employee's contributions. However, the IRS and Department of Labor have developed some rules to be sure that the employees are fairly treated. We address some of these fairness provisions as we look at some types of plans. Some key elements that these plans can pick and choose from are as follows:

*   **A profit-sharing plan can integrate with Social Security.** These types of plans allow for a smaller contribution; typically, the first tier of contributions is 3% of compensation. The higher compensated employees, including the owner, are allocated the next tier of the contribution that is split among those highly compensated employees who earn more than the Social Security wage limit for that year. The third tier of contribution is then allocated to all employees based on their wages divided by total wages. This allows the highly compensated employees to share the middle tier, which typically allocates the business owner and key employees a larger share of the employer contribution to the plan.

*   **A profit-sharing plan can integrate with Social Security and have a 401k component.** This allows the employee to also

contribute to the plan on a pretax basis. For the highly compensated employees (including the owner) to contribute the maximum deferral allowed each year, the employer would be required to contribute what is termed a *safe harbor* contribution of up to 3% to employees who participate in the plan. The safe harbor contribution is part of the requirements to be sure that all employees are benefiting from the plan. The 3% contribution across the board to all employees keeps the plan in compliance. In this type of plan, the highly compensated employee can contribute (between his or her deferral and the company contribution) the maximum allowed, which at the time of this writing is $53,000 (and $59,000 if the employee is over age 50).

- **A profit sharing plan can also be set up with an age-enhanced contribution formula.** This works well when the owner is older and most of the employees are young. This formula allows for the employer contribution to the plan to be weighted more toward those closer to retirement age.

3. **Defined Benefit Plans:** This plan funds the pension currently to an assumed monthly benefit at retirement age. For example, the employer would fund the plan to create a monthly benefit to the participants at age 65 for the rest of their lives set at a percentage of their current salary. This type of plan is used when a business has a high commitment to funding the retirement plan. The plan obligates the employer to make at least minimum predetermined funding requirements each year. Once the plan is established, it needs to stay in place for at least 3 years. The type of plan comes with a higher cost of administration because an actuary needs to run the calculations each year to determine the amount of funding to reach the monthly benefit goal. This type of plan is rarely used in small company plans because of the obligatory funding levels and the administration costs.

Many of these plan types will have specific requirements for vesting, that is, eligibility to enter the plan. Once you leave the arena of a SEP or Simple plan, you need to hire a pension consultant/administrator to make sure you do not run afoul of IRS and Department of Labor rules. Most plans other than the SEP and Simple IRA have yearly filing requirements and Actual Deferral Percentage (ADP) testing rules. These testing rules are complicated and were put in place to make sure the highly compensated owners and employees are not benefiting disproportionally compared with the rank-and-file employees. A pension consultant will help you design the plan that meets the retirement goals and funding ability of the company.

Some other features of a pension that you can write into your plan are the following:

- **Participant loans:** Participants are allowed to borrow up to $50,000 or one half of their vested plan balance, whichever is lower. Once a participant has established a loan, a mandatory repayment plan in required.

- **Roth 401k contributions:** Allows for Roth contributions, which would be posttax contributions. Contributions into a Roth 401k plan are still taxable income to the participant when they contribute; however, the benefit to them would be tax-free withdrawals (assuming all requirements are met) at retirement.

- **Automatic enrollment of new employees into 401k plans:** This feature encourages new employees to participate in the plan. Typically the plan will auto enroll employees once they reach the service eligibility date. The auto enrollment criteria and processes are defined in the company plan document and sets a percent of salary for all employees, typically 3%. Employees are allowed to opt out of the auto-enrollment, but they need to complete specific paperwork to do so.

How It All Fits Together

It is important to define your goals in setting up the retirement plan for your practice. These goals should be financially driven to meet and be aligned with your own long-term personal goals. The decision about your retirement plan should be made carefully and with input from your financial advisors (who should be carefully selected). These decisions have an impact on your long-term financial security. They deserve your full attention.

When setting up a pension (retirement) plan for your practice, it is important to seek the guidance of both your accountant and a pension consultant. Your accountant can direct you to a reputable pension consultant. The consultant should work within the parameters you set as the goals of the plan to help develop the plan that is right for your practice at the current time. The plan should also be reviewed with the pension consultant every few years to make sure the plan is still meeting the goals of the practice.

seven

Making It Work

Financial strategies alone will not guarantee a successful clinical practice. It takes a combination of such strategies, along with sound clinical judgment (Walfish & Barnett, 2009). Both need to be of high quality.

If you focus only on financial strategies and ignore clinical excellence, your professional reputation may suffer, resulting in fewer and fewer referrals. If you focus only on your clinical skills and services while ignoring financial management, you may end up in a continuous struggle to keep the lights on.

We believe a strong business model addresses both a high-quality product/service and a management infrastructure that enables those services to be offered on an ongoing basis. In this chapter, we focus on some general principles related to implementing the principles we have discussed into routine business planning and decisions.

General Principles

Keep It Simple

Having a usable system of analyzing your metrics and finances is a better choice than having a complicated system that is overwhelming and difficult to use. You can always add to and modify the system that is in place. In fact, it is often a good idea to review the system from time to time as your practice evolves and decide what is no longer needed and what new information would be of help. Additionally, you don't have to be examining the figures every day or even every week, with the exception of what is covered at the weekly oversight meeting.

Generally, monthly or even quarterly is fine. The key is finding the frequency that works for you so that you are adequately monitoring the practice and addressing things to ensure you are on course.

Don't Worry—Respect the Cycles

Many of our colleagues worry when there is a slump or many open appointments in a given week, and they worry when their schedule is packed and they do not have room to fit in another appointment. This leaves a rather narrow band, when they and Goldilocks would say, "And this is just right." Unfortunately, worrying when you're not busy enough and when you're too busy means you are spending much of your career holding on to anxiety. This is a lot of anxiety to carry for perhaps as much as 40 years! An alternative approach is to recognize that there will be ebbs and flows and to instead budget over the course of a typical year, recognizing that the weekly fluctuations are accounted for in the budget. Similarly, there are normal cycles at work both from larger economic fluctuations and smaller forces related to your type of practice and client caseload. Understanding these cycles can help you prepare for them so that you are scheduling accordingly, using spare time to market and build referral partnerships, and making sure you are avoiding burnout.

Think It Through in Advance—Crunch the Numbers

Don't guess. Consider the situation in front of you and do the math. Running your practice is no place for guesswork or making important decisions because they just "feel right." It is a place to be thoughtful and purposeful and, in many ways, "practice what you preach" to others about mindfulness and self-care (including financial self-care). When you ask yourself, what is this likely to cost and how much am I likely to make or benefit, you can judge whether the risk is worth it to you.

Right Fit the Amount of Risk

How would you feel if you heard about a practice spending thousands of dollars to convert to an electronic record, back up all their old files, and get all their clinicians tablet computers? Or let's say a practice installs a coffee shop in the lobby (Verhaagen & Gaskill, 2014). How would you feel if you heard that a practice passes up an offer to buy into a suite in a medical building? Do these ideas make sense to you, or do they seem foolhardy? There is not one right answer. Not only does the answer depend on the cost–benefit analysis, it also depends on the risk tolerance of the practice owners. The risk you are comfortable tolerating is not based on whether there is risk. Rather, it is based on your comfort level with different degrees of risk. The amount of risk needs to be aligned with your risk tolerance. From our perspective, the key is correctly fitting business decisions to your level of risk tolerance so that you are not experiencing undue anxiety (from taking excessively high risk) or undue frustration (from taking excessively low risk) that could affect your decision making and even your clinical work. That being said, it still is important to analyze each business opportunity that presents itself and not immediately dismiss it because you are risk averse. A missed opportunity could also have a long-term impact on your practice.

Common Business Decisions

Hiring Another Clinician

You're busy, a bit too busy. You have an extra clinical room in your office or times when your office is vacant and wonder, "Maybe I should hire someone so I'm not referring this work out." You know that many other clinicians hire someone and pay a percentage of what they collect. Is the going rate relevant? How do you figure out what you are going to pay? Walfish and Barnett (2009) state that the correct percentage is that which you and the employee are both willing to accept. We agree. However, we think there is even more to it than that. Here is a perfect opportunity to examine this decision from a business perspective without making it exceedingly complex:

From the income side, estimate what the person will collect from his or her starting date until he or she is at full capacity. You can estimate this by taking into account fees charged, reimbursement rates, delays in reimbursement, referral flow and hours, and weeks worked per year. Assume that the first year's income into the practice will be far less than after the person has established an optimal caseload. Next, look at your expenses both in terms of administrative overhead (e.g., billing, need for equipment, payroll taxes, health insurance and other benefits) and also what you are thinking of paying in compensation as a percentage of collected fees (if you are using this as the compensation formula). You might want to do this for the first 2 or 3 years if the first year is anticipated to be particularly low. See if this leaves any residual for profits. This can help you clearly understand what range of compensation you can afford to pay. It can also help you develop the criteria for incentive compensation (if the clinician is more productive than anticipated).

Tracking Productivity

This is often a difficult decision for practice owners. As an owner, you may be uncomfortable looking at the results and then holding your employees accountable for their productivity. Or you may be uncomfortable doing the math. In fact, measuring productivity is routine in most business environments. However, in a mental health practice, it can be nonexistent to extremely detailed and complex or anywhere in between. Nonetheless, it is important so that you can have a better understanding of the return on your investment in your clinical staff. As Chapter 3 explained, you can track hours billed, dollars collected, new clients seen, referrals generated, and any other factors that are pertinent to you. It is important to make sure that the system you have in place provides useful information and is not onerous to you or your staff. Tracking the needed information by clinician, by quarter, and by year can also help you see patterns and changes therein. This can enable you to take action before a potential problem (such as reduced caseload or loss of referrals) escalates.

Renting Office Space

This is one of the most costly business decisions that a clinician will make. It is also a decision that is made repeatedly, even if one stays in the same office space and simply renews a lease. It is a decision that easily can cost at least $10,000 to $20,000 a year and legally obligate you to $50,000 to 100,000 of expenses (remembering that a monthly rate you are quoted is a fraction of the total multiyear exposure of the lease). Yet it is a decision that is often made quickly and without taking the time to evaluate alternatives and really understand the fine-points of the lease.

Renting office space should begin with a full analysis of options and pros and cons associated with the various choices (including staying where you are if you already have space).

- Look at comparable space and obtain pricing estimates.
- Look at initial lease terms—and, as we have said before, do the math. How much is the space per foot? What are the costs of needed renovations and sound attenuation? How much is a move likely to cost? What are the benefits of being in the space that is being considered (e.g., comfort, location, proximity to referral partners, growth potential).
- Compare the best options and then begin to negotiate. Be sure to read all the terms of the lease. Are you comfortable with the respective responsibilities that are yours and the landlord's? Are you comfortable with any restrictions that may be present (e.g., regarding office availability, smoking, utilities being shut off outside of usual business hours)? Are you fully aware of all the add-ons (e.g., triple-net) and common area maintenance (CAM) charges?

All of these questions need to be addressed so that you can begin to get a sense of the value of the office you are considering and how it compares with other options in the local market. Do the analyses before you show the lease to your real estate attorney for his or her review? The business and financial aspects of this decision are significant and certainly deserve the attention of any other decision that ultimately costs tens of thousands of dollars.

Investing in Marketing

Consider the following scenarios: A community organization or medical practice invites you to give a presentation and asks if you will pay for the breakfast, lunch, or refreshments ($200–$300). This is commonly referred to as a "Lunch and Learn." A local multidisciplinary organization that relates to your niche practice has annual dues of $1,000. You get a call from someone asking you to buy production time ($2,000) so that you can host your own Internet radio show. As with other decisions, these can be examined and analyzed from a cost–benefit perspective.

Many clinicians make the mistake of simply looking at the costs of a marketing opportunity and not the potential benefits. Others get so starry-eyed about the opportunity that they overlook the cost.

Both are important. Consider the three examples we just gave. In the first, does it make sense to spend a few hundred dollars for a meal (not to mention the preparation time) to present to the organization in question? It clearly does, if there is a strong likelihood that such a presentation will ultimately lead to referrals. Just one referral would recoup your investment. Similarly, the dues to the organization can be recouped with one or two referrals. What about the Internet radio show? That might lead to opportunities, but it would be important to consider the probability of getting a good return on your investment. Is the company promising you anything in addition to "exposure"? What's that exposure worth to you? Will you be required to do additional marketing on your own to attract listeners? Who are these listeners? Will any of them be likely to use your services or recommend your services to others? How much advertising is likely to flow through the site if you are being promised a portion of that revenue? Don't simply rely on how it sounds at the time. Remember, you are the subject of a sales pitch, even if it sounds like a great opportunity. Do the math and talk to your mentors and advisors.

Lining Up Your Mentors and Advisors

Having a successful practice is often helped immensely by having trusted mentors and advisors who have more experience than you do. Although many clinicians seek legal and accounting input, they should also seek input from other mental health clinicians who have "been there, done that." Your mental health professional advisors don't have to have the same clinical specialty to have experiences and insight that could be very useful to you. They can review a contract from a functional perspective and know about certain nuances of practice that might affect the bottom line that might not be immediately evident to your lawyer or accountant (e.g., the access to heated or air-conditioned space on nights and weekends; who are the neighboring tenants and what noises or smells will come from their space). On the other hand, your accountant is critical in terms of providing tax advice and helping with business planning and financial oversight. Your accountant may point out errors in your logic or analysis. Your lawyer can find contractual issues that you are not aware of and should be fluent in local real estate law so that your interests are well represented and you are clear about the various contractual clauses large and small.

Be careful, though, about relying on professional listservs as a source of financial or practice management advice. Well-meaning colleagues (even those with national reputations) are very generous with their advice. However, they do not necessarily have the expertise that is pertinent to your particular situation. Also, they cannot possibly have a full understanding of your situation, when they only know what you posted in a few paragraphs. Lastly, do not assume that your postings on listservs are confidential. They are not. They can even be used as evidence against you if you are involved in a lawsuit.

How It All Fits Together

We believe there are many opportunities for mental health clinicians to have thriving practices. Combining sound clinical and financial management principles increases the likelihood of success. It is important to recognize that needs and opportunities exist to build a successful mental health practice with traditional insurance reimbursement, for services that fall outside the purview of managed care, or with some combination of both. Le and Walfish (2007) surveyed private practice mental health clinicians and found them to be involved in 158 niche practices activities that are all noninsurance reimbursed!

Be open to change, be open to ideas, be open to actually doing the basic math and financial calculations we have presented, and be open to using your skills in creative and new ways. By putting in place your financial infrastructure you will have a steady and accurate flow of information that can help you avoid mistakes and get the most out of your investment in your practice. You can have a personally meaningful and financially successful practice.

References

Barnett, J. E., Zimmerman, J., & Walfish, S. (2014). *The ethics of private practice: A practical guide for mental health clinicians.* New York, NY: Oxford University Press.

Crosby, L. A., & Johnson, S. L. (2006). Customer bonding: Make it memorable. *Marketing Management, 15*(4), 12.

Le, J., & Walfish, S. (2007, August). *Clinical practice strategies outside the realm of managed care: An update.* Paper presented at the meetings of the American Psychological Association, San Francisco, CA.

Verhaagen, D., & Gaskill, F. (2014). *How we built our dream practice: Innovative ideas for how to build yours.* Camp Hill, PA: TPI Press.

Walfish, S. (2001, August). *Clinical practice strategies outside the realm of managed care.* Paper presented at the meetings of the American Psychological Association, San Francisco, CA.

Walfish, S. (2010). *Earning a living outside of managed mental health care: 50 ways to expand your practice.* Washington, DC: APA Books.

Walfish, S. (2011). Practicing outside of managed care: What we can learn from our social work colleagues. *The Independent Practitioner, 30,* 34–36.

Walfish, S. & Barnett, J. (2009). *Financial success in mental health practice: Essential tools and strategies for practitioners.* Washington, DC: APA Books.

Walfish, S., McAllister, B., O'Connell, P., & Lambert, M. (2012). An investigation of self-assessment bias in mental health providers. *Psychological Reports, 110,* 639–644.

Walfish, S., Zimmerman, J., & Nordal, K. C. (in press). Building and managing a private practice. In J. C. Norcross, G. R. VandenBos, & D. K. Freedheim (Eds.), *APA handbook of clinical psychology* (5 vols.). Washington, DC: APA Books.

Glossary

Accounting System. An organized set of manual and computerized methods, procedures, and controls to record and summarize financial data that is used to make financial and management decisions.

Accounts Payable. Money a company owes to its vendors for products received or services performed.

Accounts Receivable. Money owed to the company for services performed or products sold.

Accrual method of accounting. Form of accounting that records income when billed out and expenses when actually incurred, not when actually paid.

Administrative overhead ratio. The ratio or percentage of costs of running a practice that do not include professional staff payroll or owner compensation to the income collected during the same period of time.

Asset. Any item of economic value owned by a company.

Balance sheet. Financial report that summarizes the assets, liabilities, and equity of an entity.

Budget. Projection of a future period's income and expenses.

Cash method of accounting. Form of accounting that records income when collected and expenses when paid.

Chart of accounts. A financial organizational tool that provides a listing of every account available in your accounting system.

Collection ratio. The ratio or percentage of what was actually collected to what was billed during the same period of time.

Defined benefit plan. A type of company pension plan that calculates your benefit according to your length of service and the salary earned at the time of retirement.

Defined contribution plan. A type of retirement plan in which the employer and/or employee can make contributions for the benefit of the employee.

Equity. The book value of a company. Assets minus liabilities equal equity.

Floating percentage rate. Refers to any type of debt instrument, such as a loan or credit line, that does not have a fixed rate of interest over the life of the instrument.

General ledger. A complete record of financial transactions of the entity. This is the entity's main accounting record.

Gross income. All income from whatever source.

Liability. A financial obligation that arises during the course of business operations.

Line of credit. A credit source extended to a company for use in addressing the cash flow needs of a business.

Metrics. The indices that are used to track key elements of the practice.

Net income. The income minus cost of goods sold, expenses and taxes for an accounting period.

Owner-only 401(k). A retirement plan for a single owner practice with no employees that allows for deferral contributions in addition to practice contributions.

Profit and loss statement. A financial report that summarizes the income and expenses of the practice.

Simple IRA. A savings incentive match plan for employees' individual retirement that is a type of tax-deferred employer-provided retirement plan. It allows the employer and the employees to set aside money for the employees' retirement.

Simplified employee pension (SEP). A retirement plan that an employer or self-employed individual can establish.

About the Authors

Jeffrey Zimmerman, Ph.D., ABPP, is a licensed psychologist (Connecticut and New York) and has been in independent practice for more than 30 years. He returned to solo practice in 2007 after serving as a founding and managing partner of a group practice for 22 years. He has two niche specialty practices (alternative dispute resolution for divorce and organizational consultation) in addition to a general practice. Dr. Zimmerman is a founding partner of The Practice Institute, LLC, which is dedicated to help mental health professionals build thriving practices. In 2014, Dr. Zimmerman coauthored *The Ethics of Private Practice: A Guide for Mental Health Clinicians.* He received his doctorate in clinical psychology from the University of Mississippi in 1980. Dr. Zimmerman is a past-president of the Connecticut Psychological Association and has received numerous awards including Distinguished Contribution to the Practice of Psychology from the Connecticut Psychological Association. In 2009, Dr. Zimmerman received the award of American Board of Professional Psychology specialty board certification in clinical psychology. In 2010, Dr. Zimmerman was made a fellow of the American Psychological Association in recognition of his outstanding contributions to the profession of psychology.

Diane V. Libby is a licensed certified public accountant in Connecticut with 33 years of experience in public accounting. Diane joined Adams Samartino & Co., CPAs, as a partner in 1996, coming from the regional firm Blum, Shapiro and Co., where she became a tax partner in 1990. She earned her bachelor of science degree in accountancy from Bentley College in 1982 and a master's degree in taxation from the University of Hartford in 1987. Diane is a member of the

Connecticut Society of Certified Public Accountants. Additionally, she serves on the Board of Governors for Charlotte Hungerford Hospital. She is a corporator for Brooker Memorial, Inc. and The Torrington Historical Society and also volunteers with many other civic and charitable organizations. Most of Diane's practice is centered closely around held businesses, to which she provides accounting and tax services. She works with many physician and mental health practices.

Made in the USA
Middletown, DE
23 December 2015